ZERO RISK

To my incredible kids, Brianna, Katie, Erin and Tom.
I love you all very much, and am extremely proud of you.

And to those unsung heroes who look after the homeless, to the refugees whose countries and governments have abandoned them, and to the children who face peer pressure, bullying, racial hatred or the scourge of drugs and to the parents who struggle to make their lives better.

Tony Loughran

ZERO RISK

KEEPING OTHERS SAFE
IN A DANGEROUS WORLD

echo

PUBLISHING

Shafiq Alam, Bureau Chief, Agence France-Presse, Bangladesh

Tony has made journalism safe for hundreds of reporters covering the flashpoints in the Asia–Pacific region. It's not every day that you find someone who has made such a huge contribution to make news gathering relatively safer even in war-torn places like Afghanistan, Iraq and Syria.

When I got a threat from an Al Qaeda affiliate group in Bangladesh, we had to shut down the office and for months were working from home. Tony came to our rescue. He suggested some brilliant changes in the way we covered events and how we approached security in the office. He helped me change my identity and told me to drop my long-treasured moustache as it had become a key signature feature of my facial appearance. He also brought about radical changes into how we cover protests, riots and violence in the troubled streets of Dhaka.

I am honoured and privileged to have been trained by Tony. Thanks to him, working in hostile environment is a lot easier than ever. And I am sure anyone who has met and worked with him would feel the same.

Martin Bell, OBE, British UNICEF Ambassador, former broadcast war reporter and MP

When I reported the Vietnam War in 1967 we had no body armour and no safety of medical training whatsoever. My only fieldcraft was what I had learned as a soldier. We went in on a wing and a prayer.

So it remained until the 1990s, when the Balkan wars brought us to our senses. After I had been shot up in a soft-skinned vehicle in Sarajevo in June 1992, the BBC provided us with its first armoured vehicle, a Land Rover that was formerly the property of the Royal Ulster Constabulary. We called her Miss Piggy. She saved lives. We were also equipped with body armour, which was initially too heavy. There is safety in movement as well in armour.

Tony Loughran turned that corner for us. He initiated the hostile environment courses that were necessary (I had already done mine in the real world). And he gave us the lightweight body armour that we needed (including in my case a white model to go with the lucky white suit). His is a story worth telling and worth reading.

Jeremy Bowen, International Editor, BBC News

Tony Loughran pioneered a safety culture in the news business. He adapted the skills he'd acquired in the military to the needs of journalists at the sharp end. All of us working in the field, from the Middle East to Ukraine and beyond, owe Tony a debt of thanks for making our working lives safer.

Ben Brown, journalist and news presenter, BBC News

I've been covering wars, conflicts and trouble spots for the BBC since 1988, and in that time, our safety procedures have been revolutionised, so that now we have everything from state-of-the-art body armour, to hostile environment training courses, when we are put through simulated battlefield scenarios. Tony Loughran has been a big part of that improvement; his hard work behind the scenes has contributed to much better protection for our journalists and camera teams. They say no story is worth a life, but reporters still have to report the news from difficult and dangerous places, such as Ukraine, and the challenge is always to help them do so as safely as possible.

Goraya Abdul Majeed (AFP Journalist – Pakistan Karachi / Peshawar)

It was June 2009 and I was sent to report on a Pakistan military operation against militants in the Swat Valley. When we reached our destination the soldiers at the checkpoint started to search our car and equipment. In that moment I remembered the tips taught to us on our hostile environment course – to remain alert and maintain an all-round observation on our situation. The soldiers allowed us to move forward. I remembered Mr Tony telling us at covered checkpoints to remain calm but alert.

With their AK47 rifles, the soldiers fired four shots from at our car from 30 or 40 feet away. The driver, Shafiq Ahmad, was shot in the back, and our team member Irfan was shot in his right arm. I hadn't been injured but I was shocked as everything happened so quickly. We managed to drive to safety and some local people gathered around us and offered to help.

Remembering the first aid lesson from Mr Tony, I immediately used a piece of cloth as a tourniquet to stop the flow of blood to Irfan's arm, and then packed the large wound and pressed hard on Shafiq's back. The locals then helped us get to the nearest hospital. We should have all died that day, but by the grace of Allah and Tony's medical training we survived.

Vin Ray, former BBC World News Editor and Executive Editor
The BBC has one of the biggest newsgathering operations in the world, so changing its culture is a major undertaking. But Tony Loughran did it. He combined the best training with the best equipment to create a culture where safety came first. Whether it was lightweight body armour or armoured cars, hostile environments or riot training, Tony sought and delivered them all. The impact of his work across the whole industry has been immeasurable. Put simply, Tony Loughran saved lives.

Jo Ruxton, MBE, former BBC Natural History Unit producer,
co-founder of Plastic Oceans Project
Tony was heavily involved in developing, as well as helping us to finalise, complex risk assessments at BBC's Natural History Unit when we travelled to some of the world's most remote, and sometimes dangerous, locations. On one occasion the NHU was filming the endangered Bonobo Pygmy chimpanzee in Uganda, and I was contacted by Tony to alert them that they were in danger as a notoriously ruthless freedom fighter group was taking Westerners hostage. Tony used his aviation contacts in Kenya to book in a light aircraft to extract the team, but not before they had to use GPS to measure the strip of land and clear it for the plane to land. It was Tony's system of monitoring and alerting staff in danger, which he introduced at the BBC, that saved the day.

Tony also led the way in complex diving support during the production of the iconic *Blue Planet* series and for an Antarctica shoot, he delivered a cold wilderness medical course to ensure we knew what to expect when filming in such conditions and how to anticipate, prevent, and treat any potential medical incidents. I have worked in some of the world's remote regions and dived extensively with Tony, and still rely on him for advice not only for independent filmmaking but for all my work-related travel.

Richard Sambrook, former BBC journalist and executive, Emeritus Professor in the School of Journalism, Media and Culture at Cardiff University

In the 1990s, BBC News had eight people killed on assignment in eight years. Some were shot or blown up, others were in road accidents or just unlucky. But it was an unsustainable toll. Together with the BBC's Head of Newsgathering, Chris Cramer, we set about working with Tony Loughran and his colleague Peter Hunter to change the culture of safety throughout the organisation.

Tony in particular, with his military experience, was tasked with looking at training and protocols for reporting in hostile environments and conflict zones. It was hard and painstaking work, not only to develop the right approaches but also to persuade tough, independent and sceptical reporters that they needed to change their approach. But gradually it worked and hostile environment training, security teams on location, armoured vehicles and flak jackets became standard in ways they simply had not been before. And, more importantly, Tony and his colleagues won the respect and gratitude of teams in the field who recognised their expertise and experience was saving lives.

John Simpson, World Affairs Editor, BBC News

Tony is one of the greats of the personal protection business – a man with immense experience in dangerous places, and in looking after those who go to them. I owe my life to him. During the invasion of Iraq in 2003, he went out of his way to provide me with lightweight body armour he'd specially selected. When an American plane mistakenly dropped a 1000-pound bomb on my group, killing 17 people, including our translator, a big piece of shrapnel lodged in the protective plate over my spine. Any other body armour would probably have failed to save me. So I've blessed Tony's name ever since. He's a real hero.

echo PUBLISHING

An imprint of Bonnier Books UK	Bonnier Books UK
Level 45, World Square,	4th Floor, Victoria House,
680 George Street	Bloomsbury Square
Sydney NSW 2000	London WC1B 4DA
www.echopublishing.com.au	www.bonnierbooks.co.uk
	Owned by Bonnier Books
	Sveavägen 56, Stockholm, Sweden

Echo Publishing acknowledges the traditional custodians of Country
throughout Australia. We recognise their continuing connection to land,
sea and waters. We pay our respects to Elders past and present.

This autobiography is based on the personal memories of Tony Loughran.
Every reasonable attempt to verify the facts against available documentation has
been made. All statements, interpretations and recollections expressed in the text
regarding places, people, names, dates and events remain the author's own.

First published in Australia in 2023 by Echo Publishing
Available in Great Britain as an Echo UK Book

1 3 5 7 9 10 8 6 4 2

Printed and bound in Great Britain by Clays Ltd, Elcograf S.p.A.

MIX
Paper | Supporting
responsible forestry
FSC® C018072

Editor: Anna Rogers
Cover designer: Nada Backovic
Page design and typesetting by Shaun Jury
Front cover images: White concrete wall with orange and red graffiti,
photo by Henry & Co. on Unsplash; Beige burned paper, photo by
Donald Giannatti on Unsplash; A destroyed building in a city, photo by
Mahmoud Sulaiman on Unsplash. See unsplash.com.

A CIP catalogue entry for this book is available from the British Library.

ISBN: 9781760689056 (paperback)
ISBN: 9781760687618 (ebook)

echo_publishing

echo_publishing

echopublishingaustralia

ABOUT THE AUTHOR

Tony Loughran is a global risk specialist, with over 30 years of international experience as a safety and security professional. Born in Liverpool in 1962, at 18 Tony joined the navy, as a medic, then became a commando medic in the Royal Marines. In 1991, he took on the exciting and demanding role of safety and security expert for the BBC. Among much else,  he revolutionised the way in which journalists cover conflicts, pioneering state-of-the-art body armour, improving vehicles and developing hostile environment courses that have become obligatory, and life-saving, for media personnel and others working in hazardous places. Since he moved to Australia in 2002, Tony's own security consultancy company, ZeroRisk International, has continued to involve him in high-octane assignments and adventures all over the world, from Pakistan to Afghanistan and Ukraine.

CONTENTS

PROLOGUE

'TONY, I'M AFRAID I have some rather bad news: our colleague and dear friend Sardar has been killed in Kabul.' It was late March 2014 and I had just arrived in London on business when I received a call from Marc Lavine, Hong Kong bureau chief for Agence France-Presse (AFP). It felt as if the world had slowed down and I'd suddenly gone deaf. Sardar had always looked after me when I worked in Afghanistan. Everyone regarded him as bulletproof; surely this couldn't be true. Marc then asked me if I could drop everything and fly to Kabul to find out what had really happened and to be with the team at the office.

As always, when I arrived in Kabul and cleared all three airport terminal gates, Daud was there to greet me with a big bear hug: 'Tony, it's good that you're here. We've missed you.' The ride to the AFP house was quiet, punctuated only by the constant tooting of horns and the roar of motorbikes and scooters passing our vehicle. Daud was clearly in shock. He had been very close to Sadar and this was a great loss. Once we were inside the compound I hugged the guards, drivers and staff; it felt like coming home. I then stepped inside the office and right in front of me was Sardar's reclining chair and pictures of his wife and kids on the desk. Ben Sheppard, the

Kabul bureau chief, entered the room. 'I'm going to miss that lion of a man and the pleasure of waking him when he'd dozed off in the afternoon.'

Almost immediately, Marc Lavine joined us on a phone hook-up from Hong Kong and mentioned that he'd obtained a preliminary police report. This is what appeared to have happened. About 6 p.m. on Thursday 20 March, Sardar, his wife and three children were sitting at a table in the Serena Hotel when three Taliban gunmen opened fire on them and others dining there that night. (There was a fourth man whose gun jammed.) Nine people were killed, including Sardar, his wife Humaira, his six-year-old daughter Nelofsar and his elder son, five-year-old Omar. His younger son, two-year-old Abuzar, was hit several times and went into a coma, but survived. The main target was thought to be a high-level Indian delegation visiting weeks before the presidential election, which was marred by fresh violence in the Afghan capital.

Information on the case was held by the police and all we could deduce from talking to witnesses was that the gunmen, all young kids, had observed the security guard force at the front of the hotel scanning down the body of every visitor with a security wand but stopping short at the ankles. Armed with this information, the gunmen had secreted small pistols in the hollowed-out heels and soles of their footwear. They'd walked the bullets through and hidden them in the toilet. By all accounts, they couldn't disguise their nervousness as they sat at a table. When one Indian diner next to them saw them rising with their pistols, he threw bottles at them. Sardar moved towards the gunmen, trying to protect his wife, but was shot, along with his family.

This attack happened just days after the assassination of Swedish journalist Nils Horner, who was shot dead in the streets of Kabul on Tuesday 11th. Nils had hoped to speak to survivors of a January

Taliban attack at the Taverna du Liban in the Wazir Akbar Khan area of Kabul, home to many foreign embassies and major news organisations. The only connection between the two men was that Sardar helped Nils with logistics – a driver, a vehicle, a translator. A number of people I spoke to couldn't help but think that Sardar may have been surveilled by the gunmen and this killing was related to Nils' investigation.

I visited a number of local Kabul hospitals and clinics and conducted interviews with hospital staff so I could establish which were the safest hospitals in the city and, more importantly, which would admit expats, because there weren't many. I'd interviewed a number of journalists who had all told me the horrific story of a number of expat staff who had been injured in a bomb blast but were refused admittance by some hospitals. One casualty had bled to death because no help was available. My other concern was that some of the hospitals were used extensively by Taliban to treat their fighters in the adjoining Ghazni and Wardak provinces.

I'd arranged to interview medical staff at one hospital on the outskirts of Kabul. Daud dropped me off at a large and imposing metal security door with a sliding window slot, just like you see in the movies. Through his car window, and in Pashtun, Daud explained who we were and they opened the door and gestured for me to come inside. Daud was then abruptly told to go. I started to realise that something was wrong: this was a strange hospital and I was stuck in the middle of nowhere. I was taken into a badly painted room covered in bullet holes and my phone was grabbed. Three men entered, one a tall guy with a glass eye, one armed with an AK47 and another holding a radio. They started with a good cop, bad cop routine, asking me questions. I knew what they were capable of: they had the capacity to kidnap me, drive me out of town and incarcerate me in a chamber the size of a water tank and

3

leave me there for months. Often, they slashed people's Achilles tendons so they couldn't run. I could feel my life flashing by. My heart raced and I could sense the blood draining from my body. Shock was kicking in and I needed to gain control of the situation.

There were four rooms in a line, with interconnecting doors. The last room was nearest the street. On previous occasions, entering Kabul, I had been given a pistol when working with security contractors, but often couldn't reveal this to anyone. In this scenario it became a guessing game for the people I was facing – were they Taliban? – as to whether I was carrying a weapon. But I managed to get myself out by sheer willpower and speed, moving my body hard and fast at each doorway and then waiting for the large steel main gate to open before making a dash for it. As soon as I got outside and saw Daud waiting in the traffic, I let out a huge sigh of relief. As we drove back to the base, I hardly uttered a word. Daud told me how helpless he had felt when he was ushered away. He suspected that all was not well but was powerless to do anything. As we left, I noticed a few cars parked close to the brick walls of the hospital and couldn't help but think that I was destined for one of them and a long spell in a remote mountain region. Daud had been circling in his vehicle until he saw me and I ran out. His loyalty was incredible. I owed him my life and to this day he remains a very dear friend.

CHAPTER 1

THE BOY FROM BOOTLE

MY EXPOSURE TO high risk started in the dark, cold back streets of Bootle, Liverpool, where I was born in 1962. My father was a stevedore, working on the docks. My mother was a docker's widow, thanks to Dad's long work shifts and even longer hours at the pub. Dad inherited his alcoholic gene from his father who, like all good Irishmen in those days, drank each glass as if it was his last and fought just because he could.

My dad, Brian Vincent Loughran, had a tough life. As a child, he'd paint his ankles and feet white because he didn't own socks and had to borrow his sister's blouse for school. There simply weren't enough clothes for everyone. His two older brothers were offered scholarships to St Mary's College, a private Catholic school. My father was intelligent enough to follow in their footsteps but the money in the Loughran household had dried up and his wages were needed. I believe it was this that placed a massive chip on his shoulder and made him bitter about and resentful of anyone else who succeeded. Having been told that his private education was not going to happen, Dad left school at 14 to begin a series of jobs, including one as a blacksmith striker, which meant he beat the living daylights out of metal on an anvil all day long. When he left there at 17, to join the Merchant Navy, he was 1.65 metres tall and weighed 69 kilos and his reference read 'although small is very strong'. Dad left Liverpool for training in Bristol with a friend but after the first night woke up to find his mate had gone. He stuck it out, though, and sailed to many places, including Africa, the United States and Japan, where he witnessed the nuclear devastation at Hiroshima. I can remember him showing me the photographs. In New York he placed his hand on the Empire State Building, then the tallest building in the world.

I knew about Dad's strength from experience. When I was turning 13, he set me a series of strength tests that included bending a 15-centimetre nail with both hands, lifting a chair up from the floor with one hand and crushing a beer bottle top in half with just two fingers. These tests often began at 11 p.m. or midnight when he'd return from the pub and finished when he passed out about 1.30 a.m. When he got home, he'd take his stinking boots off at the doorstep and walk noisily through the house. Of course, I then had to get up at 7 o'clock to get ready for school while Dad slept off the night before and had virtually no recollection of what had taken place. When I was older, he blamed my poor education results on lack of study, but I could never concentrate properly thanks to constantly disrupted sleep.

Throughout my teenage years I experienced a terrible emotional tug of war with my father as I constantly sought his love and affection and, most of all, the praise that never came. He was, I think, caught in a generational time warp; he came from a very poor family and, as they say in Liverpool, was 'dragged up and not brought up'. Despite this, however, he could laugh in the face of adversity and, like me and my daughter Brianna, was often the life and soul of any get-together. It was not uncommon for him to break into a song by Frank Sinatra or his all-time favourite, Nat King Cole.

When Dad wasn't in his Mersey Docks gear – the obligatory donkey jacket, jeans and steel toe-capped boots – he was slipping on his Marks & Spencer trousers, clean shirt and paisley tie. The ritual was always the same: a glance in the mirror, a tightening of the tie and a sweep back of the black greased hair and he was ready for an afternoon, evening, or both, at St Benet's Club. The final piece of Dad's going out dress code was the small leg iron he'd inherited from a huge fall on the docks – 6 metres down a hatch with a belly full of lunchtime beer – that had resulted in a very badly smashed ankle. We'd wander home from school not knowing if Dad would be there or had decided to head to one of his mates' houses for an extra few beers.

When Dad was sober, he was a very different person, quiet, thoughtful and engaging, which confused the hell out of me, Mum and my siblings. This was the father we wanted but couldn't have because his mind and body were consumed by insecurities, anxieties and drink.

Despite this, though, Dad had a wonderful sense of humour. One day, in prime position in our back garden, he built a fishpond out of an old council washbasin and filled it with plants and three large goldfish. After the third day, to Dad's puzzlement, one of the goldfish disappeared. The mystery was solved later that afternoon when a neighbour knocked on our door and held up a bowl with our goldfish swimming in it: his cat had brought it home. 'Brian,' he said, 'I think this is yours.' Dad didn't miss a beat. Staring at the fish, he said, 'How many times have I told you about going out without telling me?' He then thanked the neighbour before slamming the door and shouting, so that the confused neighbour could hear, 'You're grounded.'

***

My mother, Irene, was born in Liverpool, the daughter of Queenie and big Tom Spofforth, a towering figure at 1.93 metres and a John Wayne lookalike. Mum idolised him but when she was only 21, he died of a heart attack right in front of her. Queenie was destroyed by her husband's death, and after spending a year in mourning and not eating very much, she died of malnutrition brought on by deep sorrow. After both her parents were gone, Mum lived with her five brothers, Reggie, Ronnie, Eric, Sid and Kenny, in the family house in Ballantyne Grove, Bootle, and they all stayed very close until she met and married Dad.

When I was small, I remember Mum being full of laughter and energy but as time went by this side disappeared, mainly due to Dad's drinking and erratic behaviour. Mum did well to keep this from us but after many vicious fights with my drink-fuelled father, she became determined to have a better life, and pushed for us to get a council house. She even saved up enough money later to fulfil a long-held dream of going to Australia to see her brother Ronnie. Mum is small in stature and looks rather like the late Queen Elizabeth. She has boundless energy and enthusiasm and engages with anyone and everyone. I've often been told, 'You're so lucky. I wish she was my mum.'

Although I was two years older than my brother Jeff, we were like twins and were often referred to as the Krays, not because we were criminals but because we were so tight. Early on, though, we fought all the time. Mum puts it down to the fact that when I was very young, and Jeff was still in a pram, I bit his thumb and ran off. Jeff got his own back, though, and would often snitch on me. Once, after he'd told Dad that I'd lied to him about stealing something, my conscience got the better of me and I told Dad the truth. He just looked up, called me a barefaced liar and said, 'Get thee behind me, Satan.' My relationship with Dad was beginning its downward spiral but Jeff's was on the up and up.

Both of us were sporty but he was the one who got onto the cross-country team, who was the fastest sprinter, who made it to the local school football team security trials for Blackpool and Sheffield United. He often appeared in magazines. I hardly ever made it to the school first team, but that never stopped me from bragging to my mates' girlfriends and families that Jeff Loughran was my brother. This praise was to be returned much later in life when I heard from friends that Jeff would spend hours talking in glowing terms about his big brother.

In our later teen years, we sounded exactly the same on the phone and had a lot of fun talking to each other's girlfriends and admirers. Jeff, by now a hulk of a guy, had all the girls running after him. He didn't know until much later that I got to know them intimately by pretending to be him and broke a few hearts by promising much and delivering zippo. We shared a bedroom until the day I left to join the Royal Navy. Jeff always had my back, providing an alibi on our many thieving trips or when we'd cause mischief by breaking windows or setting fire to bus stops.

Angela, my sister, was extremely studious, neat and tidy – the polar opposite to Jeff and me. She inherited the sensible gene. Mum was fiercely protected by her brothers, but Jeff and I had little time for our girly sis. We'd often marvel at how she applied herself at school and flourished there: 'Education Breath' was our nickname for her. She then attended Matlock Teachers' Training College, which led to a much-cherished degree. Angela was always a saver and had a piggy bank in which she'd deposit copious bank notes and coins. But Jeff and I were aware of this little treasure trove and regularly turned it upside down to extract a fair bit to finance our own vices. I really didn't see my sister for many years as I left home when I was 18 and we'd only spend time together at obligatory family gatherings. Sadly, this gap, plus the fact that our careers were on totally separate trajectories, contributed to us growing apart.

***

My father travelled to see me after I was born in Walton Hospital during one of the coldest winters in Liverpool history. With knee-deep snow and driving Siberian winds roaring over the Pennines, he braved 1.9-degree Celsius temperatures and a perilous 4.5-kilometre journey on a scooter to meet his firstborn. He had not been allowed anywhere near the hospital's labour room; a special room for expectant local fathers was set up in the Merton Hotel, about 400 metres away from my grandad's house in Fernhill Road, just off the Liverpool Dock Road, where my parents were living, to await the news. As you can imagine, none of the dads ever complained about this arrangement.

The Fernhill Road house was a battered old place. We were so poor that the living room was virtually empty – no carpet, wallpaper or ornaments, just a large wooden desk with a single lightbulb hanging over the table. People taking a shortcut home by walking down the alleyway that ran along the back of our house would sometimes get a glimpse of my grandad sitting on the outdoor shitter, reading the *Liverpool Echo* with his trousers around his ankles and false leg on full display. Grandad didn't care and flicked the occasional V sign at the gobby neighbours. When I asked him why he placed torn-up strips of the *Daily Mail* on the loo roll holder, he replied, 'It gives me great pleasure to slide the Tory rag across my arse in the morning. The only thing true about that paper is the date.' This was my introduction to politics. I haven't looked at toilet paper the same way since.

I lived there with Mum, Dad and my paternal grandad, Big Mick Loughran, who had hands like shovels and a Lee Marvin look about him. My nan, Margaret Loughran, had left him many years before because of his moody and violent outbursts. I've often been told by my uncles how neighbours would hear a loud scream, followed by my nan exiting the house with a small tomahawk axe flying through the air above her head. Forced to go through his pockets for money, she would choose the times when he was sleeping off an afternoon's drinking at the Merton; it must have been the rattle of coins that woke him up. She sought shelter in the Lord and Southport's St Mary's church and became the cleaning lady for the church and annexe buildings.

Grandad wasted most of his life and talent due to drink, hard labour and the docks, but I looked up to him and he was often the only company I had since Mum and Dad worked full time. He seemed like a warrior to me, with his granite jaw, craggy, hard face and those massive hands, which were apparently a godsend, since he came from a long line of boxers. He was quirky, very intelligent – he could complete a crossword in seconds – and he let me play with his wooden leg under the dining table.

I found out my grandad was dying of cancer after he'd been coughing blood for weeks and had gone off his food. He'd lost a lot of weight and his impish smile had disappeared. One afternoon Uncle Pete, a writer and the most imaginative of Dad's family, decided he'd take me and my siblings to visit Grandad in hospital while my father was at work. An emaciated, shrivelled man, who looked vaguely familiar, sat upright in bed, shouting at the top of his voice, 'Get those bloody kids out of here. Whatever possessed you to bring them in?'

My nan was highly strung, dedicating all her waking hours to the Catholic church. Music was everything to her – she missed out on a music scholarship to Oxford; her family couldn't afford food, let alone an education – and she taught me to love it. As a kid I was in the school choir and very nearly obtained a scholarship with the Vienna Boys' Choir; my Uncle Pete tried to persuade my parents to send me there. I loved listening to my nan playing the banjo, ukulele and miniature piano. I developed a good ear for picking out tunes on the guitar and playing them over and over. My two younger daughters, Katie and Erin, have inherited this ability. When I was four, my nan gave me an odd little musical instrument called a stylophone. (My brother once labelled it 'the Stephen Hawking voice box'.) It had an electronic keyboard you could hold in one hand and glide a plastic pen across to hit the notes. I stood there in awe as my nan produced a rendition of 'Danny Boy'.

***

In 1967 we got lucky. We left the hardships of Bootle for a new house in the pristine village of Netherton, an overspill town for some of Liverpool's slums. According to family lore, Dad was tipped off that the Mayor of Bootle, Veronica Bray, was to attend a ball at the council chamber. Dad and Uncle Gerard went along and between them started working the floor, with the aim of schmoozing the mayor. Dad had heard she had an eye for handsome men and saw this as a one-way ticket out of Shitsville. No sooner was he dancing with her than Dad started crying on her shoulder, telling her that life in Bootle was unbearable and his young wife deserved better. Drenched in my father's tears, Veronica insisted that he go to the top of Netherton's housing list. It was a sweet victory for a working-class stevedore with hardly two pennies to rub together.

In Netherton I could see colours other than black or grey, there were modest gardens and picket fences and our front door had no axe marks in it. When we first arrived, I needed to go to the toilet but I couldn't see one in the empty backyard. In sheer desperation, I peed onto the small fence that divided our property from the neighbour's. I felt an icy stare from above: a woman in a hair net was looking down at me from an upstairs window with an expression of sheer disgust on her face.

The new house felt spacious, compared with the shoebox in Fernhill Road. I could smell fresh timber in some rooms as there were no carpets. As she climbed the stairs and turned right, Mum was beaming. 'Well, what do you think?' she said, pointing to an indoor toilet and a very modern and bright bathroom. 'But Mum ...' 'It's simply heaven, isn't it?' I didn't have the heart to tell her I'd just got caught by the neighbour taking a piss. It was as if we'd been given back our lives. Everything in Bootle was dark, dingy, smelly and hostile. Our new address, Truro Avenue, was light and bright; even the name sounded posh and uplifting. Later Mum saw to it that we bought this council house, thanks to Margaret Thatcher and the scheme she introduced in 1980 that forced local authorities to sell such homes at a discounted price if requested.

The first winter we were there, some local kids and I built a snowman at the top of the street. As soon as we'd finished, we built another snowman and another, until the entire street was blocked off with a wall of icy men in metre-deep snow. One of the lads winked at me and said, 'Brilliant, we'll create a small opening, cut down two trees and lay them across it. Then we'll then charge everyone a penny to enter the street.' This was a great idea: we were set to make a fortune. Unfortunately, after we'd made a brilliant start and had encouraging looks from the locals, one car stopped to find out what was going on. A huge guy got out and asked to place his penny in my collection bag himself, only to steal the bag from me and deliver a blow to the side of my face. He bashed down our wall and drove through.

I ran home in tears and told my sad story to Grandad and my Uncle Gerard, Dad's eldest brother, who were visiting. At first Grandad smiled at the cheek of our scheme, but his mood turned to rage when he heard that I'd been hit. After he'd strapped on his wooden leg, he and Uncle Gerard, whom he called Uncle Filth, went in search of my assailant. They tried in vain as the weather turned really nasty and snow was banking up all around. Not wanting to let this one go, Uncle Gerard came back the following day and set up a little fox hole with me at the top of our road. We stayed there from 5 until 9 p.m.

Finally, I recognised the car from the day before. As it rolled towards us, my uncle stepped out and asked the man for help because I was stuck in the snow. The man got out and, to my disbelief, my uncle delivered the famous Loughran two jabs with his right fist. There was a large thump as the guy hit the icy path. My uncle leant over him: 'The next time I'll hit you softer and I'll get this boy to finish you off.' He then fished inside the man's trouser pockets and pulled out a wad of cash. He kept the notes himself and threw me all the pennies. In the future I would often watch my brother delivering the same family move on many a thug.

Uncle Gerard was a Clint Eastwood lookalike, very suave and debonair, and great company, though as he got older his favourite friend was Villa Maria chardonnay from New Zealand. Like Dad, Gerard started life poor, kicking around the streets of Liverpool. During his mid to late twenties, he was in and out of relationships and really couldn't settle. I loved his company and found out more than most what made him tick. Like Dad's other brother,

Peter, he was well read and very intelligent. He was the first of the Loughran kids to gain a scholarship to attend the prestigious St Mary's College and by all accounts came away with a good set of qualifications.

* * *

Most kids in the area went to St Benet's, a Catholic school with the motto 'With Jesus we learn, love and laugh'. They left off what happened if you stepped out of line: 'We deliver the cane, strap or slipper.' I only got caned once by our headmaster. I'd finally made it onto the school football team and was placed as goalie. The score was 2–2 against St Raymond's but I couldn't wait any longer for a pee. As I urinated behind the posts all I heard was a whooshing sound, as the ball flew past my head and burst the back of the net, followed by a blood-curdling scream from the games teacher. Lifting me up by my ear, he dragged me to his office and threw me in his stockroom: 'I'll deal with you later, you little shit.'

I took the liberty of checking out his briefcase and devouring the contents of his lunchbox. Then my classmate Tony Quillan appeared, also in trouble. My eye caught a pair of saggy old undies, which I picked up with a miniature statue of Our Lady and spun around until I could see the dark shit stain running through the middle. Then Our Lady catapulted the teacher's undies at great speed towards the ceiling fan, just as their owner entered the room. All hell broke loose. I didn't just get caned, I got slippered and given 3000 lines. Many years later, my skin crawled when I learnt that this teacher had been convicted of sex offences.

As a young kid, I considered our street long and wide and the house and people huge. We had acres of room to play in and there was a huge triangle-shaped playing area, which became my go-to space when things got rough or when my parents needed time on their own. Opposite the triangle was a long skinny alleyway leading to an enclosed plot of land that housed all the residents' garages and an enormous electrical pylon. My first instinct, as with anything tall and dangerous, was to climb it. Using a dockyard rope I found at the side of a garage, I got to the second cross-brace and tied the biggest knot I could manage before dropping the length of the rope to the ground. I was a bit worried about the constant fizz and spark from the overhead electrical conductors but more worried about being caught by my dad. It was worth the risk, though. With a huge plank of wood threaded onto the bottom of the rope, we could swing it to the corner of the pylon, then hop on and swing to the other side. It was like a human kebab with so many people leaping on the rope. The skin on your hands would be shredded with the force of holding on.

The 'back hills' (aka our secret garage area) become our gangland den. Here we'd store our stolen booty and spare parts for motorbikes. We didn't experiment with drugs, but we puffed on loosies, cigarettes made from the dog-end tobacco discarded by the factory. Many kids spent their lunch money on five loosies and a Sally Lunn iced bun from Sayers cake shop. It was from our HQ, too, that we hatched a plan to get up early and sneak out, riding our bikes for as far and as long as possible. This turned out to be 30 kilometres to Southport, the poshest and most affluent part of northern Liverpool – a brilliant area for thieving.

Front and centre of the Netherton gang was my brother Jeff. Fiercely loyal and inspirational, he was forever dishing out dares to check your level of commitment. One was split the kipper, which involved two people standing opposite each other, feet apart. The idea was to throw a knife between your opponent's feet, which were gradually moved closer together and nearer the knife. You played until eventually the knife penetrated a shoe. As we realised later, we were at a disadvantage. Our shoes were 'plazzy' (plastic), not leather. To this day I still bear the scars of split the kipper.

To keep everyone in check, we had St Benet's Catholic priest, Father Vincent 'Ahem' O'Reilly. The nickname was bestowed by our gang. When he read mass, often drunk, he'd forget chunks and give a resounding and frequent 'ahem'. When I got older and took on a part-time job at St Benet's Catholic Club, I often stepped over Father Ahem as he lay prone behind the bar, clutching a bottle of Cutty Sark whisky. 'Jeez,' said Dad, 'all the money that club's raking in and all His Eminence can swig is Cutty Sark. It's that bad, you couldn't even give it away on the docks.'

When Dad had a shift that ended at 5 p.m. he would often take a small diversion to the Merton, from where he'd down a number of Tetley's beers before staggering home. His arrival usually coincided with us finishing dinner, which meant we had a perfect view of Dad swaying to and fro, trying to open the front door. Having passed the lock test, he would swerve confidently past the outstretched cat, slump onto the green plastic couch as if he'd been hit by a sniper, then lapse into a beer-induced coma.

As kids, our bathing ritual was to shower by connecting two rubber tubes to the hot and cold taps, firmly tied on by a pair of Mum's old tights. One night, after showering and changing into his pyjamas, my brother slipped downstairs to prank Dad. Rolling up his trouser leg, he drew a huge phallic symbol on his calf. Dad never flinched and we giggled at this brilliant stunt. Not long after, Father Ahem, doing his weekly rounds on his bike, dropped in for a scotch. Mum, embarrassed that Dad was lying horizontal in the living room, reeking of Johnnie Walker and snoring loudly, nudged him to get up and greet our guest. Father Ahem walked into the living room just as Dad let out an almighty snort. His attempt to sit up revealed Jeff's masterpiece. Mum stared at Father Ahem, Father Ahem stared at Mum and Dad stared at his leg before shouting, 'Kids!'

CHAPTER 2
FROM THE MERSEY TO MALTA

MY UNCLE PETE was one of the most influential figures in my life. He was fit and constantly challenged me physically and mentally, which helped me immensely in later years. In 1971, when I was nine, after enduring a really bad time with my father where we just couldn't see eye to eye and I couldn't believe a word he was telling me, Uncle Pete decided the best solution was to take me away from Liverpool, show me how to live independently and reveal the importance of travel and adventure. I was to go to Malta, where he lived and wrote novels, including *The Train Ride*, *The Third Beast*, *Kristina*, *Jacqui* and, in 1983, *Dearest*, which was described on the cover as 'the most gruesome book you've ever read'.

Malta was a great escape, an experience that completely altered my view of the world. Just leaving Liverpool's dull overcast skies behind me and boarding a train to London to stay for four glorious nights at my uncle's flat in Sanderstead changed my world. I was smitten by the life of the commuter and the sights and sounds of a bustling city. London also introduced me to spaghetti and elderflower wine. Yes, even though I was only nine, my uncle introduced me to alcohol.

The first night, he pulled out a small wooden box and then told me to jump in the car as he had something to show me. Uncle Pete was always doing the unexpected and loved to break rules and so naturally I couldn't wait to see what crazy little adventure he had in store. When we arrived at Shirley Park, only about 10 minutes away, the light had faded and the night sounds were starting. It was so quiet that the cooing of a dove could be faintly heard over the beautiful evening song of a lark.

My uncle laid the wooden box on the ground, then said, 'What I'm about to show you goes no further and you mustn't tell your parents, do you hear me?' After I said, 'Yes, yes ... of course', he opened the box and pulled out two large objects draped in white towelling. As the fabric fell away, I couldn't believe my eyes. Right there before me were two old flintlock pistols, the kind you see in the *Pirates of the Caribbean* movies. Pete looked me directly in the eye. 'I'm going to teach you how to load these, and if you do a good job we'll see where we go from there. First you hold the pistol like this, completely upright. Then you take this little bag of gunpowder and using this rod you ram it into the barrel as hard as you can. Next you take this little lead ball and ram that in as hard as you can. Now take this cap and place it over this little spiky bit here to the side of the pistol ... and now you're *live* and you *must not* go anywhere near the trigger. Always point the pistol down at the ground away from your foot, and listen to everything I have to say.'

I was shaking with fear and excitement and couldn't believe that I had a real loaded gun in my hand. 'Now watch me closely,' said my uncle, as he pulled his pistol up and took aim at a pigeon on an old English oak. He steadied himself, took one last look around to make sure no one was nearby and then, with a click and a flash of the percussion cap, there was an almighty bang as the lead shot hit the pigeon. Feathers went flying in all directions and you must have been able to hear the echo far and wide. Uncle Pete looked at me and said, 'And now we wait until another fatter pigeon lands on that branch and it's your turn.'

I could hardly believe what I was hearing. Sure enough, 30 minutes later the biggest, fattest mother of all pigeons landed right in the fork of a tree. Without flinching, I raised the heavy pistol and stared at the bird. I wasted no time: I pulled the trigger back, cocked the weapon and squeezed the trigger so hard that my finger ached. Without warning, the pistol ejected a huge flame and the sound that followed was deafening. Even worse, the heavy pistol was too powerful for me and I toppled over onto the ground. Much to my surprise, I'd actually winged the bird and my uncle summoned me to finish it off by wringing its neck. This was my introduction to hunting and I was deeply grateful to Pete for showing me the ropes.

The following day we packed, ready to leave later for Gatwick and an overnight flight to Malta. Finally we were on our way. We caught the train out of London, then sat in a very empty airport before boarding our flight. After walking across the tarmac, we climbed the stairs to the forward door, where my uncle smiled at the rather attractive flight attendant, who said, 'My, what a beautiful boy! It must be nice having a son.' Without missing a beat, Pete said, 'Yes, he's a very special and lucky lad', to which she replied, 'Yes, he is, to have such a handsome dad.' I should have realised at this point that I was his babe magnet; he used this kind of line a few times when we were in Malta.

This was my first time abroad and my first time on a plane, a BEA Vickers Vanguard with twin propellors on each side that made an incredible buzzing noise as the engines roared along at 36,000 feet. My head barely reaching the window, I sat there gasping at the fluffy white clouds that rolled and tumbled by. Were these really clouds? I'd only seen them as cotton wool blobs from the ground; now they looked solid enough to walk on. The journey seemed to last forever but in truth it was only a two-hour flight from London. I nervously experienced my first aircraft landing, gripping my seat hard as the plane descended and taxied to a complete stop on the runway at Luqa.

Nothing could have prepared me for the intense gust of hot air swirling around me when they opened the aircraft door. I couldn't see much as it was 5.30 in the morning but I knew I was somewhere very special as I felt the Mediterranean heat blasting my face. I felt almost as if I couldn't breathe: it was like landing on some strange fiery planet. Palm trees swayed in the warm breeze.

None of the shops were open as we cruised in a taxi straight to the Sliema waterfront. My uncle knew where to be and that was Joe's Bar and Café. My first sunrise in Malta was spectacular. A huge orange disc burst up from the horizon and sprayed golden light onto the white marble and limestone of the villas. I was mesmerised. To release me from this trance, my uncle told me to fish my togs out of my small suitcase. Half an hour after leaving the airport, we were taking our first swim in the balmy Mediterranean Sea among some extremely tanned people. That vision of clear aqua blue water is ingrained in my memory. I always thought the ocean was brown; the River Mersey in Liverpool was the only water I knew. This was very different to cracking the ice and going for a frozen dip in the rat-infested Leeds and Liverpool Canal. When I opened my eyes under water I saw schools of fish darting in and out of my legs, not plastic bags often stuffed with unwanted pets.

When we got out of the water, the morning heat dried us off in seconds. From a car hire shop, we took possession of a very small Triumph Herald. I never had the will or the right words to ask what we were doing next. I was just following the Pied Piper. My life back home had vanished. I didn't once felt homesick.

As we rounded the corner, I saw a sign for Sliema Flats and a small corner shop busy with kids buying Coca-Cola in the old-style traditional bottles. After travelling a little further up a sandstone street, we reached our destination at No. 18 St Mary Flats. As I looked up at this tall block I could hear the cacophony of kids going about their daily life, punctuated only by a mama bellowing orders at the top of her beautiful Maltese voice.

'Come on,' said Uncle Pete when we got inside, 'let's get you out of these long trousers and jumper and put on the shorts and T-shirt your mum packed.' With that I was transformed into one of the local boys and I would stay in shorts, togs and T-shirts for the entire trip. Then my uncle told me we were going next door to meet a family he'd known since he was 19, when he first came to Malta.

What happened next really blew me away, as one child after the other streamed out to greet me with a warm and inviting hello. After the tenth child, there was a succession of grandchildren, then Lulu, the older daughter whom my uncle had the hots for, then Mama Sansone, pulling her apron down, touching her short brown hair. She walked straight up to me, squeezed my cheek and wrapped her arms around me. I thought I'd died and gone to heaven. Without missing a beat, Martin, Stephen and Chris Sansone, all about four to six years older than me, invited me into their basement to play Subbuteo or tabletop football. My jaw hit the floor as I saw a full stadium with thousands of miniature spectators and boxes upon boxes of all the teams from the Serie A Italian League and a few from the English Premier League. My eye, of course, was drawn to the Liverpool team, which I adopted for the entire time I was there.

Life in Malta was idyllic. Each morning I'd walk up the road with a threepenny coin, which I passed through a hole in the wall to be replaced with a giant warm and crispy fresh loaf of bread wrapped in newspaper. I never saw anyone who worked there but I'd hear voices saying, 'Innglish Beatle Boy, enjoy your day.' After this, I headed back to the flat and started my daily chores of sweeping and mopping the floor. Then I'd clean the rooftop balcony, where you could sleep at night and stare out over Sliema and Valletta.

After I'd finished my tasks, the Sansone boys would all be waiting for me with small spear guns, masks, snorkel and fins. We'd run down to the Sliema front and dive straight into the water. I learnt to catch octopuses, which we sold to Joe, as he paid good prices for a fresh catch. Not only was I now initiated as a fisherman but as a budding businessman too. I also discovered the joys of freediving.

Malta continued to be one beautiful dream. Uncle Pete and I made several trips to historic landmarks like the miracle Church of the Assumption of Our Lady in Mosta, where, on 9 April 1942, two German bombs fell during a service packed with 250 people but failed to detonate. The first hit the dome, ricocheted and landed on the floor of the church. The second just missed the left-hand side of the façade. Both were defused and thrown into the sea, but a replica of the first bomb was still on display. There were also night-time Catholic fiestas with fireworks, sweets and cakes.

One day my uncle told me I should pack a small bag as we were going to a Maltese Island called Gozo to see a friend of his who was also a writer. As we sat in a café beside the turquoise green sea, my uncle showed me the book his friend had written. I looked at the title, *The Cruel Sea*, and thought that the sea had been very kind to me. Within minutes a giant of a man with a shock of swept-back white hair was standing over me and I was introduced to Nicholas Monsarrat. As he and my uncle talked about all the places they loved back home in the UK, and other novels and authors they held in high esteem, I became bored and joined a group of local island boys to show off my newly acquired diving skills. We all had immense fun diving from the headland into the surf until a rogue wave caught me and three others and dumped us into the ocean on a fast outgoing tide. My uncle, seeing everything in slow motion, was thinking how he was going to break the news to my parents that I'd been swept away. All of a sudden, four Maltese men who were repairing their boats stripped off their clothes and dived straight into the sea and carried us on their backs to safety. Nicholas Monsarrat looked at me shivering with fear next to my uncle and said, 'Now you know why we call it the cruel sea. Be careful, young man.'

I would visit my uncle in Malta again over the years, but nothing ever erased or surpassed that extraordinary first visit.

CHAPTER 3
THE REALLY HARD YEARS

COMING BACK FROM my time in Malta was difficult. I had to exchange a sunny, happy, laid-back place for the dark, small grey environment of Liverpool. When I walked down the street with my uncle, my own mother hardly recognised me: my hair had been bleached blond and I had a deep tan. I told Mum to open a clear Nescafé coffee jar I'd brought back with me. Inside was a dead octopus pickled in methylated spirits – it represented my Maltese life. I had presents for everyone, especially big slabs of Maltese nougat. I felt like the prodigal son as I handed them out. Another gift was some holy water, which I kept in a plastic bottle on the mantelpiece until I accidentally drank it when I was drunk one night, aged 18. The best present of all was a crystal necklace, which I saved till last and gave to Mum.

It felt as if Dad shunned me after Malta, probably because he hadn't had such an opportunity when he was a kid. It seemed as though he knew he couldn't give me what my Uncle Pete was offering and so somehow stopped being a father and let himself become consumed by life on the docks and drinking. He was clearly in awe of my trip but never really asked me anything about my time away. My uncle had given me the chance to be independent

27

– he'd let me do the food shopping in Malta – and to grow as a boy. I believe the easy relationship between us made my father resentful and quite jealous.

He picked on my sister, Angela, resentful that she had a better education and was a genius at English and maths. She was the only one smart enough to challenge him on some of his poorly researched statements, which left him struggling with his identity and authority. Jeff was the apple of his eye, the sporting hero, the larrikin, the jokester. He wasn't perfect, though: once, when I was about 12, he volleyed a ball through the house, smashing a bottle of Dad's best whisky. We cleaned the mess up but Dad found out and demanded we come clean. Jeff blamed it on me and my sister and watched in silence as Dad battered us all the way up the stairs, throwing us into the bedroom. Jeff never owned up.

The word 'love' was uttered once after nine pints of bitter but for the most part there was tension and disappointment. Dad was jealous of my hard-working mother, who in 1999 would be awarded an MBE for services as a revenue assistant at Her Majesty's Board of Inland Revenue. He hated that she earnt more than him and had a social life and was smart. They moved in cycles where he withdrew and drank a lot more, and Mum would walk off and find somewhere else to sleep. Over time their relationship unravelled bitterly.

Once my parents had a terrible row, in which Dad accused Mum of just about everything. It got so bad that when I looked down the stairs, I saw Dad passing a large breadknife to Mum, insisting she could end it right now by stabbing him. Had it not been for the intervention of my eccentric grandmother walking between them, raising her hands and singing 'Ave Maria', I dread to think what would have happened. Although I see the macabre humour of Nan's attempt at peacekeeping, the horrifying image remains powerful. Mum and my sister left the house and Jeff and I rushed out to find them. Mum's brother, Kenny, discovered them heading to a friend's home. Jeff and I were left to try and get back to bed. Dad had passed out, completely oblivious to what he'd said and done and deeply remorseful the following day.

I avoided Dad as much as possible. I'd stay out longer with my friends to avoid his drunken tirades. I found one of the best friends anyone could have in a giant of a guy, Kev Conlan. It was Kev who realised that the situation in my household was bad, and he would often ask his mother, Mrs C as I called her, if I could stay over. She had 10 kids and her husband had died very early on but she just got on with life. For me, she was like a surrogate mum.

As an alcoholic, my dad was the typical Jekyll and Hyde. At the pub he played the great guy, the good listener, the valued friend. At home late at night he'd be staggering and either funny or aggressive, and in the morning often retching and coughing up blood. He developed a large stomach ulcer and had to have a partial gastrectomy, which rendered him medically unfit for work but didn't stop him drinking and smoking 60 unfiltered cigarettes a day. Following the operation, Mum threw his best mate out of the hospital room after he hooked Dad's IV drip up to a bottle of Johnnie Walker. It was touch-and-go for a while if Dad would actually survive the prank.

Christmas could be tough. It was hard watching your mates get bikes and other great presents while we just had to be grateful we got anything at all. My aunt used to kindly knit us tank tops (sleeveless jumpers) instead but she was nearly blind and always managed to get our sizes wrong. Christmas Eve was quiet in our house, not cheerful or festive. Dad would only eventually arrive home about 11 p.m. from the club and usually spent Christmas Day nursing a hangover.

The Christmas I was 12, though, I had good reason to believe we were all getting bicycles. It was the era of the cool Chopper bicycle, with the fat tyres, and everyone wanted to own one. On Christmas Eve Dad got home early from the pub, though still drunk, and wrapped up two bikes. While lowering them carefully down the stairs one at a time, he slipped and ended up at the bottom, tangled up with one of the bikes, knocking himself unconscious and waking the house. Dad obliterated the illusion of Santa for my 10-year-old brother and nine-year-old sister.

I was all excited when I unwrapped the surviving bike on Christmas Day, but what I found was a stolen Dunelt off the docks, with a massive saddle big enough to fit two arses and really embarrassing handlebars. There had in fact been only one Chopper, intended for Jeff. The Dunelt looked fit for a vicar, not a scally from Liverpool. I couldn't hide my disappointment. When I told Dad I couldn't even reach the pedals, he said, 'You'll grow into it. Ride the bike sitting on the crossbar.' I refused as I could already feel the cold steel splitting my nuts. On Boxing Day morning Dad got his mate to build wooden blocks and coach-bolt them onto the pedals. When you were riding it looked as if you were wearing stilts. Fortunately, that day, a local gang threw a stick through the spokes of my front wheel while I was travelling at speed. The stick slammed against the front forks, catapulting me through the air along with the heavy bike, which slammed itself against a tree that I missed by millimetres. My street cred was intact once more.

One year Jeff received cool Adidas football boots for his birthday in February, so when March rolled around, a boot-shaped parcel allowed me to get my hopes up. But instead of the Franz Beckenbauer Adidas football boots I'd desperately hoped for, I received a very old pair of rugby boots, with ankle protection and green wooden studs on the base. Once again I couldn't mask my disappointment. I blurted through a river of tears that I was expecting Adidas boots. Dad said, 'What? Are you telling me they're not Adidas?' I said that no, Adidas boots had three stripes and these had four. Without missing a beat, he put his cigarette to the corner of his mouth and ripped one stripe off the side of each boot. 'There you go, only three stripes. Now they're Adidas.' When, as a sub on the school football team, I got a chance to play, the minute I started to run, the sole of my right boot fell off and I spent the rest of the game going down the wing to the sound of slapping leather and the huge roar of laughter from the sidelines. I felt like the circus clown with the oversized shoes.

***

One day Dad announced that he thought it was best if I applied for a scholarship to prestigious St Mary's. To achieve this, I had to sit an entrance test, which I dreaded. I really enjoyed school but, thanks to various disruptions, I'd never grasped basic maths and English skills. During and straight after the test I knew I'd failed miserably. I hid this from my parents but one warm summer's afternoon the little brown envelope arrived and I sat on the step waiting for Dad to come limping down the street from the pub. Without a word, I held up the envelope. After reading the contents, he prodded me really hard with his walking stick and said, 'You're a failure. You can't even get this right', and didn't speak to me for the next two days. Mum was my saviour. She looked me in the eye and said, 'Well, St Thomas Aquinas it is then. I'm sure you'll do well there.' St Mary's was never discussed again.

St Thomas Aquinas, where I started secondary school in 1972, was a place where gangs, bullies and nutters reigned supreme, a place where I fought to survive and came away with one handy qualification: how to defend myself against a smashed bottle, a golf club or a knife. I needed new uniforms, stationery and books that we really couldn't afford, but somehow Mum pulled everything together for my first day. There were even new leather shoes, Clark's Commandos, with animal prints on the soles and a built-in compass in the heels – in the middle of Liverpool? And it meant that I couldn't get up to any mischief now as there would be a tell-tale print at the scene of the crime.

When I tried on my new uniform, Mum said, 'Be very careful. We don't have the money to replace it.' Famous last words. On the first day of school we were in the art room, which had huge plate-glass windows. I got into a fight with another kid, shoved him through the window and dived after him into the broken glass. Not only did I get my first public caning from the headmaster, but I'd ripped my brand-new blazer. Mum stitched it up as best she could. Dad gave me a hiding and I was grounded for a month.

St Tommy's was considered the hardest of Liverpool's schools and its education league tables were appalling. The teachers ruled with an iron fist, and they had to. It wasn't uncommon for a pupil to assault a teacher or, even worse, to be in the classroom and witness an unhappy parent barge through the door with a barking rottweiler before launching a vicious attack on the teacher.

I didn't get off to a great start and everything deteriorated from there. Ten months later, I was walking to school with mates, approaching the canal bridge, when I ran out in front of a car and copped abuse from the female driver. I gave her the fingers and laughed it off with my friends. At assembly, after we'd said prayers and sung our compulsory Catholic hymns, the headmaster, a short Welshman with eyebrows that wouldn't look out of place on a woolly mammoth, barked an order for everyone to stay exactly where they were and remain still. At that point, my world fell apart: entering the hall was the woman I'd insulted, here to do a formal identity parade. I tried hard to look ahead when she cruised past but the rip in my jacket gave the game away. I was told to appear on stage, where the headmaster announced that his wife had that morning been subjected to disgusting verbal abuse from Loughran and two others. After passing the sentence, six cuts on each hand and six on the arse, he made me move to the front of the stage, where he dispensed the punishment with his bamboo cane, striking harder than usual. His wife stared unblinkingly at me the whole time.

At the end of each school year we'd be handed a thin brown envelope containing our school report. One year I dropped mine into the Leeds and Liverpool Canal, hoping my dreadful results would disintegrate in the mud around a sunken set of car tyres, a Tesco shopping trolley or a used condom. But a gust of wind blew it onto the cycle track underneath St Benet's Bridge. One of Dad's mates, who happened to be fishing there, swung by our house and delivered my soggy shit report, resulting in an array of punishments no kid should ever endure.

It was the summer of 1978 and we'd completed all our O-Level subjects of maths, English, geography and history. I knew I'd bombed out. Only a week before our tests we sat a mock multiple choice physics paper, for which I managed to get two out of 30. The teacher informed the class that 'Loughran has done so badly that one mark was for getting the date right. I could have given an ape a pen and he would have got more correct answers.'

Before results came out, I escaped to the Lake District, my go-to place, and enjoyed a few glorious weeks of camping and hiking. It was a sobering return remembering the O-Level results were to be published in the school hall on Monday for all to see. Luckily, Mum didn't come to school so I went along with my brother, Jeff. I stared up at the wooden notice board and saw a string of U's and one C next to my name. U stood for ungraded, slightly worse than F for failure. Walking home, my head bowed low, I turned desperately to Jeff for brotherly advice. 'Just tell Mum that U means higher than a Grade A and the U stands for guaranteed a university place.' Brilliant! I delivered this news to my mother, who gave me a huge hug. I still remember looking over her right shoulder and winking at my brother standing in the kitchen. He reciprocated by giving me a huge thumbs-up and a beaming smile.

One day, however, Mum came home looking shocked, embarrassed and completely dejected. Outside Woollies she'd met Mrs Ryan, who'd mentioned that her son, Super Swot Alan, had got straight A's. Quick as a flash Mum said, 'Oh, never mind. Alan will just have to do better at his A-Levels. Tony got straight U's, which is higher than an A and it means he's fast-tracked to university.' Mrs Ryan delivered the truth-bomb and my red-faced mother pulled her scarf up over her face and head and began the walk of shame from the shops back to our house.

***

As we got older, I realised our area lacked much for kids to do besides getting into mischief. They kicked around at night, they had no sense of purpose and nowhere to go. Getting into gangs was inevitable. We'd scoop up dog poo and hide it under a random neighbour's door mat. We'd then set fire to the mat and hide in a tree to gleefully watch the results. The neighbour would come out and stamp on the mat to kill the flame, then walk the dog poo back inside on his shoes. We'd kill ourselves laughing and only had to wait another minute to see the door open and a shit-marked rug flung out, with the victim shaking his fist at the sky and saying, 'Fecking kids! I'll get you if it's the last thing I ever do.'

Breaking into shops was common. We'd steal cigarettes or sweets and store the booty on top of the flat-roofed power station at the end of the street. When Labour Prime Minister Harold Wilson, who never forgot his northern roots, came to officially cut the ribbon and unveil a plaque declaring the Marion Square shopping centre open, we dared each other to see what we could steal from him in broad daylight. My mate Barry won by asking the pipe-smoking PM for a photograph and swiping his pen from his left-hand breast pocket during the process. Later that night, the pen was raffled off down at the Eden Vale pub. My mates were also able to steal three televisions from Radio Rentals while the police and the mayor and the shopowners stood around watching as the plaque was unveiled. Later that month a television commercial aired in our region, with the slogan, 'Not happy with your TV? You should have gone to Radio Rentals.' Well, the boys did and were very satisfied.

The Eden Vale pub at the end of Marion Square was then the roughest, most dangerous place in Liverpool. It was the watering hole for local gangs, everything was sold there in broad daylight and kids sneaked in to steal beer dregs from drunk dockers. Eden Vale was Dad's regular: he sat in the same spot every night and kept his special pint glass behind the bar. Little did he know that we'd all been drinking in this pub since the age of 14. We knew what time he'd be there and just went around the back.

In addition to petty theft and neighbourhood mischief, the Netherton Boot Boy gang were partial to a full-on fight. Our rivals were in nearby Crosby, an area considered a bit posher than ours. It had a public swimming pool and we used to cycle there in our Doc Marten boots for a swim. One day, while locking my bike up, I got smacked over the back of the head with a golf club by the Crosby Boot Boys. My gash required stitches. On and on the gang rivalry raged in the neighbourhood.

I was a young boy when I saw a dead body for the first time. It was a friend of Dad's, a crane driver on the docks, who lived around the corner. Thinking it would be a great idea to toughen me up and prepare me for life, Dad made me go along to view the body lying in an open coffin on a trestle. After that I thought I was prepared to face anything, but it wasn't until my knockaround buddy and neighbour, Debbie Brown, died in a car accident when I was about 15 that life really started to mean something. Everyone knew that Debbie struggled with drink and drugs, but no one could believe that she'd be killed by walking straight into an oncoming fast car. Everyone loved Debbie. She was so funny and disliked anyone posh or up themselves: she taught me how to do the rude finger and how to deliver the right facial expression to make it more effective. I'd spoken to her only an hour before she was killed; this was my first taste of how unpredictable life was. Her funeral was attended by many, though her father made just a fleeting appearance before heading off for a number of pints at the Eden Vale Pub.

Around the same time, our close friendship group took another hit. Some of us were heading out to Marion Square and we decided to call around to Jacquie Witter's house, which was a few streets away from mine. Jacquie was a lovely girl, very quiet, but very bright with a wicked sense of humour, and she loved hanging around with our gang from Truro Avenue. Her mum told us that Jacquie was upstairs sleeping as she'd been complaining of a dreadful headache for some time. I was told to go upstairs and knock on the door to wake her, but there was no answer. I knocked several times, and then I was joined by her mother, who asked me to move aside. It was then, as she opened the door, that I realised something was wrong: Jacquie was lying there, still, with her eyes wide open.

CHAPTER 4
THE LEAVING OF LIVERPOOL

AFTER I BOMBED in all my O-Levels, I was persuaded to move to Warwick Bolam High School and resit some of my subjects while also studying for my A-Levels. Although committed to school, I needed money to fund my social lifestyle and secured a part-time evening job at the Our Lady of Walsingham Catholic Club. It was anything but ladylike. My job, as the pot lad, was to collect empty used pint glasses and put them on the bar. It wasn't long before I was entrenched in a local scam. When a drunk punter wasn't looking, you'd take his full pint back to the bar; it was then served again to someone else and you'd get half the price of what the beer was bought for. It was like being one of Fagin's boys in *Oliver Twist*, fleecing people in the taverns of old London.

The sticky carpets, filth, heavy smoke and beer stench became a second home to me and it wasn't long before the club's cast of characters were a second family. Big Jimmy, on the door, was a former Second World War POW who was marched from Greece to the top of Italy under dreadful conditions. He and his fellow captives played a game of counting the number of lice in their hair; whoever had the most would win a scrap of bread from the others. There's no doubt Jimmy's war had left him with psychological scars. He'd stand there, night after night, with a vacant stare on his face, eating crisps. He mostly stayed quiet but was useful for pulling people apart when the fights started as he never made a fuss and after throwing someone through a door he'd adjust his filthy raincoat, which he always wore, even on the hottest of days, and carry on eating crisps. One day he looked at me after he'd ejected a drunk and said, 'You know, the trouble with that lot is they never say please or thank you.' I wasn't sure if he was serious or if this was his way of making a joke. All I knew was to stay in his good books.

One night the band was on and Doris was on the stage singing the song Al Jolson made famous, 'Rock-a-bye Your Baby with a Dixie Melody'. Unbeknown to her, her husband Tommy had been sleeping with someone else and it was just at the finale of the song, where her voice climbed to the top of her range, that she clocked the other woman coming into the club, arm in arm with Tommy. Quick as a flash, she dragged the other woman up onto the stage by her hair. Ernie, the manager, whose tall skinny frame and gaunt look reminded me of an undertaker, tried to break them up, but it was like throwing a Christian to the lions. He emerged covered in scratches, with patches of skin and hair missing and a bleeding eye. As he passed me he muttered, 'Let that be a lesson to you – never get involved in a two-woman scrap. Now get me a very large whisky.'

My world really opened up when Ernie said, 'You're good enough to work behind the bar.' I was lightning quick with orders despite the fact I could barely add up. I had a method of looking at the price of the drink, rounding it up, then taking a certain amount off the total. I got to know people by their drink and named them so. 'Black and Tan' (Guinness and ale) might come in on a Friday night for his usual, and 'LG' (Large Glenfiddich) would be in a bit later on. At that age I'd work till 11 or 12 at night and often stay after for what was called a lock-in – drinking with the locals and staff. By 17 I was a super fast barman, easily able to serve three customers at once. I'd leave pints pouring while collecting other bottles and get the next drink ready. Ernie recognised this and one day said to me, 'You're really good. I'm going to give you your own private bar' and he did.

Local business owner Paul Walsh also recognised my skills and was a real mentor to me. One day he offered me a place in his central heating company. I was there for a year and loved it. It was a brilliant place to work and I really started to grow, but although I was holding down two jobs, which paid well, I started worrying about my future. I had no qualifications (I only obtained one O-Level, in geography) and my time spent at Warwick Bolam was wasted as it proved more of a social hangout centre. I continued to play the class clown and spent more time betting on the horses at the nearby shopping centre than being in class.

In March 1980 I turned 18 and asked myself, 'Is this really what I want my life to be?' I'd had an interview with the National Girobank for a filing job. The interview was a speed test to see how fast I could file an excess of paperwork associated with cheque processing but I was so slow that I didn't get the job. It was a blessing in disguise: I would have been heading for a life of boredom, if I had worked there. I actually wrote to the Giro five years later and thanked them.

Then one Friday night in the bar, the son of one of Dad's mates waltzed in, broad chested and bronzed, with a woman on each arm. I watched, mesmerised, as he bought them drinks, then learnt he'd joined the navy and was on leave from a stint in the Mediterranean. As I slowly poured his beer, I thought to myself, 'That's what I want to do.' I suspected I was still on a police watchlist for stealing motorbikes with my mates and breaking them down for parts, and so the navy looked like my one-way ticket out of here. On a hot summer's day in May, without telling my parents, I slipped off to

Victoria Square in Liverpool to take the entry test for the Royal Navy. I was sweating profusely and really didn't think I'd get in so afterwards I put it out of my mind completely.

***

A few months after I'd completed the test, my mate Kev and I went camping in the Lake District, which to me is still one of the most beautiful places on earth. It was great to be outdoors, climbing and adventuring instead of getting up to mischief in Liverpool. One morning I walked to the nearest phone box and called my parents, who told me there was a brown envelope at home for me marked 'On Her Majesty's Service'. Immediately they asked me if I'd been in any trouble, because this type of correspondence was usually from the police. By the time I got home I'd forgotten all about the letter, but there it was waiting for me behind the clock on the mantelpiece. It read 'Congratulations, you have been accepted into the Royal Navy. Please attend an interview on 16th August.' I put the envelope on the floor and looked at my parents, who were clearly waiting for bad news. 'What have you done now, you soft shite?' Dad asked.

I felt happy in the knowledge that I'd be getting out of Liverpool. I'd had enough, it was time, I was ready for what lay ahead. I didn't have a suit for the interview and so Mum asked her seamstress friend to make me one. It ended up two sizes too big.

The interview and your test results dictate what you do in the navy. When I turned up on the day, I hadn't a clue what role I wanted. In the waiting room I met a guy from Liverpool called John Crohn. It turned out that his grandfather used to drink with my dad. John said, 'Do you fancy being a medic? It's like a ship's doctor', and that was it for me. The day we left Liverpool, we caught the train together. It felt good having someone to start out with.

From a young age I'd faced up to the reality of death. I'd come to rely, too, on the endless support of my close friends, like Kev, during my troubled teen years and when dealing with my dad. Among them was Paul Donaldson, one of my best mates in Liverpool, cool and very funny. Paul joined the Metropolitan Police and really loved it but many of those I grew up with were stuck in their lives. They'd go to the pub or clubbing on the weekend and go to work during the week. To me it seemed that folks in Liverpool became lost or they up and left forever. I didn't realise the full enormity of this at the time, but during the 1980s, approximately 12,000 people were leaving the city each year: it was one of the largest exoduses since the Second World War. I could have stayed at home and followed the groove, but my trip to Malta years before had given me a taste of what was out there in the world. I wanted a challenge; I wanted to shoot for the stars.

Today, when I'm lecturing at various functions and universities, colleges or schools, I tell the audience, 'I'd rather spend one day as a tiger than a hundred years as a sheep.' Life is for the living and those who don't grab life's opportunities may regret it later. Or maybe they don't and are content to live a more predictable, safe life. We also need these people to keep the cogs of society turning, but I chose to be a tiger and my chance was about to come.

***

I woke the morning of 21 January 1981 with my guts twisted in knots. I was about to start my new life in the navy and I worried I'd mess it up, as I had my schooling. But it was time to travel in the footsteps of so many men in my family – travellers, who lived life on the edge. Maybe it was our Irish/Viking blood. Dad had seen the world, and my Uncle Ronnie had been torpedoed at sea during the war, not once but twice. Now it was my turn. Dad was never one for fond farewells, and so I was shocked when he offered to travel by bus with me to Lime Street Station and see me off. I still can't figure out if he was offering support or just making sure I'd finally gone for good.

As we wandered up the road, I saw a few friends and said goodbye, then watched them kick a football off into the distance. It felt as if I was seeing things with fresh eyes for the first time. Kids entering the supermarket with trench coats ready for a good day's thievery. Kids on the corner of Truro Avenue, one giving me a slow motion 'Fuck off' sign, the other laughing at Dad limping. Staring out the dirty bus window, I knew I'd just dodged a spell in a remand centre or prison. I was leaving behind the smashed bus shed windows we destroyed for a dare and the stolen chocolate and ciggies.

At the station, the prostitutes who used to give us sweets and chewing gum were outside the Penny Farthing Pub as usual. I was suddenly grateful for a free-range childhood roaming up to 25 or 40 kilometres a day. And for the traditions I was farewelling, the good and bad times, the endless nights playing Knock and Run, watching the Eden Vale pub spill out at closing time where drunken dockers, often in freezing weather, staggered out in a cloud of Woodbine cigarette smoke and lies and excuses to their wives.

Dad passed me a brown paper bag, instructing me to open it on the train. As I looked out the train window at him one last time, he spotted me and raised his walking stick. Curiosity got the better of me and I unrolled the top of the paper bag. He'd given me a chocolate Wagon Wheel biscuit, 10 Woodbine cigarettes and a scrunched-up note. Munching on the biscuit, and pocketing the Woodbines, which I later sold to a guy from London, I read:

No mon, no fun, Your son.
Too bad, how sad, Your dad.

It was an expression that meant, 'Suck it up and keep going in the face of hardship.' It was his way of giving support and encouragement. It meant a lot to me.

**

As we journeyed south, John Crohn and I watched kids get on board at each station, carrying one small suitcase as instructed. Some wore shirts and ties, which fascinated us. As they say in Liverpool, 'What do you call a Scouser in a suit?' 'The accused.' Arriving at the modern, clean and upbeat Plymouth station was a culture shock after dark, grim Liverpool. The people bustling about their day looked happier. There were more cars in the streets, the temperature was warmer, there was almost a holiday feel to the air.

We were met by a huge, tall petty officer with a thick Grizzly Adams beard and steely gaze. He ushered us towards a bus with 'ROYAL NAVY' emblazoned along both sides. The final leg of the journey was achieved by staying on the bus and boarding the Torpoint ferry to cross the River Tamar to the naval base, HMS *Raleigh*, for six weeks of basic training. As we listened to the creak and clank of ferry chains from our bus seats up high, John muttered, 'I always thought the sea was brown', referring to the Mersey back home, and we exchanged a grin as we sat with nervously clenched knuckles. The bus, with 25 boys on board, was getting smelly thanks to sweat and farts. I could hear a kid sobbing but I felt only excitement. I knew my life would change and I was so ready for it. For a boy from a family who didn't own a car and had to thumb a lift to go anywhere, it was amazing just to be here.

43

As we entered the vastness of the HMS *Raleigh* training grounds, cannon were going off, people were marching around like toy soldiers; a ginger-haired kid was on his hands and knees polishing grooves on the steps with a toothbrush. Later we discovered this was a common naval punishment. Off the bus now, we lined up for a head count in the main car park. A military officer handed us a piece of paper and yelled out our official number from his records, then 'Do you register?', expecting prompt responses. I could immediately see they were picking the weakest links. If your response wasn't swift or loud enough, you'd be screamed at: 'Down for 10 push-ups.' Welcome to the navy.

We were instructed to carry our suitcase in our left hand, with the other hand at a right angle, snapping sharply with every footfall. Marching to our block, we were a comical, ragtag outfit. Some kids, too poor to own a suitcase, had their belongings in plastic bags and at least one spilt his gear en route. Thankfully my parents had lent me a decent brown case. It had a broken zip so I had elastic straps to keep it shut. Dad had used it when he went to train for the Merchant Navy all those years ago and it is still in my possession.

At the dorm block we saw that we would be sleeping side by side, 30 beds crammed in one dorm with zero privacy. Every sound, sight, smell was on display. We were directed to put down our suitcases and stand to the right side of a bed with heels and toes together. Kids were shivering with anticipation or fear. A round-shouldered guy directly opposite me got a whack in the stomach for insolently chewing gum. His gum flew out near me. He had to lie on the floor to retrieve it and put it back in his mouth. I watched him crawl to the bin and spit it out.

The naval regulations were issued to every recruit on day one. We were instructed to read and study this manual inside and out. 'Read it as if you were reading a letter from your lover' was the command, which went over most of our heads. The size of the book, 25 by 20 centimetres, was the dimensions a recruit must fold his kit down to. A fraction longer or shorter and they'd throw the offending items, generally your socks and undies, out the window and make you crawl down to retrieve them.

After getting the kit issued to us, we laid it and our clothing on the bed. Our next task was to arrange it in the shape of the Union Jack: two white vests, two underpants, two red vests, two blue underpants. A small sewing kit with needles and cotton, a black and white shoe shine kit, a two-piece razor with a shaving brush and some other bits and pieces. It was difficult for the poorer kids, whose second-hand white vests were yellow or grey.

Our cohort was a real mixture and everyone gravitated towards kids with a similar background, in my case those who carried flick knives and showed some street smarts. The kids who suffered the most during the training course were those whose parents had wrapped them in cotton wool and those from farms. When I say kids, some were up to 30 years of age; some had been to prison or had faced something significant in their lives. Everyone got a nickname. The navy was a great leveller and it spared no one. It really was survival of the fittest.

By the first night my long hair had been removed in favour of a buzz cut that showed all my childhood scars. The barber charged 50 pence, which we had been instructed to bring him. We had to salute him at the start and finish of the cut, then wade through a floor full of hair to the door. My buzz cut made me look really hard and evil. As I turned off my light, a Portsmouth guy, John Pickering, 10 years my senior, asked me if I was okay. 'Yeah, why do you want to know?' A plumber and electrician before the navy, John was appointed class leader. He made me the deputy and we had each other's back through the course, sharing notes and experiences. He has been a huge influence in my life and we've remained close. I am godfather, or the Don, to his beautiful daughter Carly.

That first night in the dorm, any fears were on public display. The youngest in the room was 16 but we could hear a few kids crying and whimpering. One had his rosary beads out and was praying. There were humorous moments as well. When a kid cried out, 'I want my mum', and another wearily replied, 'I've had your mum, so don't worry about it and shut the fuck up', he got some laughs. Some kids brought slippers to wear with pyjamas; some didn't even own pyjamas so wore underpants. Some outfits were pink, striped or very interesting. One Chinese kid wore *Kung Fu Charlie Brown* pyjamas. My pyjamas, bought by Mum at Marks and Spencer, were the kind that needed ironing.

Bulling boots and keeping your uniform tidy is a cornerstone of the navy experience. You hold a boot in your left hand, pick up the polish and spit on the boot. Rub a rag in circles, then repeat. It takes two hours until you get a shine and it's not achieved until you actually see your face in it. If you overdo it, the polish cracks or the shine blurs and you have to start all over again. During my time there a guy bought bottles of American shoe shine called Pledge and did a roaring trade. You just poured the solution on your boot and when it dried it gave an instant waxed shine.

Our kit list included two sets of boots, plimsolls, a navy blue collar and a plastic hat, two sets of mess tins and some vouchers to use at the Navy Army Airforce Institutes (NAAFI). There was a fight for the laundry room every morning and evening as our clothes had to be inspection-ready for the following day. Most crucially, the navy set us up with our very own bank account number so part of our pay could be sent home. Dispatching £47 a month gave us a feeling of responsibility. I kept doing this for 10 years.

Humans adapt to survive, and the dorm room was a study in

adaptation. We shared tips and divided up jobs based on skill and specialisation. Someone was adept at tying the cap tally (special bow on the left side); someone else would do the washing. We discovered that operating as a team works much better, and it was really encouraged by the navy. We stuck up for each other and grew closer. We learnt certain tricks for getting around nightly inspections. If we had accidentally left a full rubbish bin, someone would discreetly knock on the door and slide the bin next door during the inspection. We would put sheets out the window and slide down them to alert the next dorm what the inspection team was looking for.

Inspections generated punishments and there were plenty of opportunities. To make the bed properly, the sheets had to be folded so tightly around the bed that the 10 pence we carried in our pocket would bounce into the air when dropped. One guy was almost blind and wore thick beer-bottle glasses. At one inspection the petty officer went over his bed and picked up his underpants, which had huge skid marks on them. As a punishment he was cruelly told to wear them on his head as a mask for the weekend, with the skid running vertically across his face. On Sunday night the undies had to be cleaned and ready for the next inspection. We rallied around, finding him bleach for his undies, but psychologically the damage was done.

The parade square is the Mecca of any naval base, and nobody can so much as spit, walk or slouch while on it. The lieutenant, 'Shovel Face', was a boxer with the flattest face we'd ever seen. One day we actually saw him shouting, 'Left, right, left, right' while riding his bicycle across the parade ground, his left hand firmly on the handlebar and his right arm conducting in sync with the downward press of the pedal. Every time we marched we had to be as upright as an ironing board. He'd scream, 'Six weeks with me, I'm going to whip you into shape and if I don't I'll fuck you up for life. Your choice, ladies.' The times we had to practise parade or drill got pretty ruthless and chaotic as you could hear a cacophony of orders being barked at each class. We had six classes, each with 30 kids, all named after famous seamen or battles.

Some kids struggled with the physical challenges while others breezed through. One of the challenges was scaling a 10-metre rope, using just your arms. It was a test you had to pass and if you didn't, you'd have to do it again and again until you did. Training together was bonding. Some went on to be radio operators, cooks, chefs and aircraft engineers. It was a real privilege to be a part of something bigger than ourselves. They kept us busy with passing out tests; I was doing well and thriving. Basic training wasn't that bad for me. Mum had already taught me to clean, iron and sew, so I found that side of naval life easy.

***

At the end of basic training, our class, Frobisher, was awarded the guard of honour, which was bestowed on the class that was the best on the drill square at the navy's prestigious passing out parade. We were overjoyed. We would carry a silver SLR (self-loading rifle) weighing about 4 kilos, very heavy, and wear white ankle gaiters, white gloves and a white belt with a tabard that housed our steel bayonet. It was a big deal: the mayor came from Plymouth and everyone's families were arriving. I hadn't heard back from Dad after a phone call a few weeks before. 'I'm not sure what's going to happen,' said Dad. 'Your mother's gone to visit her brother in Australia.'

The day started with a big breakfast before we went to the armoury to clean the silver bayonet until you could see your face in it. Our uniforms were inspected to check we had the mandatory seven creases at the bottom of our trousers, representing the seven seas of the world. We came marching out of the drill shed in unison; stepping off with the first cannon roar, we turned sharp right, moving as one. With every sharp left and right the tacks on the base of our steel boots clattered like thunder. Lifting our weapons high in the air, we brought them down every time our heels hit the ground. The parents clapped and shouted. I felt an immense sense of achievement as we slammed to a halt. Then it was time for the prize giving and my name was called: I won a class prize, a book called *Ships Through the Ages*. A set of cannon then fired blank rounds, marking the passing out of all 30 in our class. We saluted until the 'Fall out' shout, turned to the right and threw our hats in the air, the final tradition, as proud parents rushed towards us. Pocket cameras flashed; the crowd thronged around me.

One by one, my classmates left the parade square, dispersing for their special weekend leave, allowed to wear civvies for the first time in weeks. To be left there, as one of those with no family present, was devastating. I couldn't understand how they had missed my moment, my achievement, and yet in a bizarre way it helped to make me the man I am today. I learnt the value of independence and how to remain strong in face of adversity. I have struggled to find a photo of that passing out parade. Had any one of my family been there, this would have been a different story.

John Pickering took me under his wing for the afternoon. His wife Tricia bought me a beer at the NAAFI and stayed for a couple of drinks and a steak and ale pie before they all headed off to Plymouth. I felt nervous about calling my parents. Maybe they had a good reason and someone was in the hospital. It took me until Sunday night to work up to ringing. When Dad answered, his voice was gravelly; he'd had a lot to drink.

'Dad, why didn't you come down?'

'Sorry son, Tetley's Bitter was doing a special for the weekend, 10 pence less each pint, and I couldn't miss out on that opportunity. Besides, I had to help with the Pass the Pint Liverpool to Manchester charity run.'

This meant only one thing to me: more free beer and an excuse for him not to travel south. I found it terribly sad. Dad was gripped by an addictive need for alcohol. Only with many drinks under his belt could he find the confidence and the will to step outside the safety of the house. It was time for me to push on and make something of myself.

CHAPTER 5
MEDIC AND COMMANDO

THE NEXT PHASE of training was medical school in Portsmouth. Basic training, the physical side, had suited me perfectly, but this looming academic training was terrifying. If you failed two tests you'd be sent home from the navy with your tail between your legs.

Portsmouth is a great maritime town and as the navy bus pulled in John Crohn, John Pickering and I were excited to see huge ships. After dropping off people at various navy establishments along the way, we pulled in next to HMS *Dolphin*, the submarine training school. When I saw the 30-metre escape tower used in training by submariners, part of me wondered if I'd joined the wrong branch. I'd learnt to dive in Malta and that kind of stuff excited me. But my mate kicked me and said, 'You don't want to spend your career in a cast-iron coffin.' The submariner recruits got off the bus and we headed straight for the Royal Navy Hospital Haslar at Gosport, on a peninsula on the western side of Portsmouth, built in 1753 to care for sailors of the fleet.

As we poured off the bus and were rounded up on the parade square in front of an accommodation block, I could smell everyone's nerves. Standing in a neat line in front of the chief petty officer who'd shouted us to attention, we looked directly up to see a naked guy standing at the window. As he started singing songs from The Smiths, the officer whipped around to yell at him, 'Bostock, get out of there, you filthy animal.' Dave Bostock, a medical laboratory technician, had a strong sense of humour and this was his way of giving two fingers to the establishment. Dave left the navy a couple of years later, but we became close friends and he had a huge influence on me. We both liked the same kind of comedy, particularly Laurel and Hardy, and would often quote them word for word over the phone. Dave's favourite was the sketch in which dopey Stan is on the phone and keeps repeating over and again, 'You don't say, you don't say' before hanging up. When Ollie asks, 'Who was that?', Stan retorts, 'I don't know, they wouldn't say.'

After a long stint at university, Dave headed back to his hometown of Nantwich and took up digs with his parents. I didn't know, but he suffered from depression, though his life was made so much better when he met beautiful, intelligent Angie and her son. One day at the BBC, where I was then working, a call came through from Dave's dad Brydon with the terrible news that Dave was dead. While walking Angie's son home from school he'd been hit by a kid joyriding in a car. After the news sank in, I walked out of the office and into a bar in Shepherd's Bush and drank anything I could get my hands on. Dave was only 36.

Coming from HMS *Raleigh*, where everything was so razor sharp, and where you couldn't get away with anything, I liked the more relaxed Haslar campus already, though I recognised that this could also be my downfall. I was put in a cabin in a brand-new medical training block with three other guys who had also been through basic training over the past six months. After a dormitory, it was a novelty to share a smaller mess with just four people. We could see the ocean from our bunks. Inspection rounds began that night, but they weren't as intense. The medical officer in charge would spot a blanket out of order and say, 'I don't expect to see that again.'

The Royal Navy Medical School was the most prestigious in the world and it trained you to work alone as the medic or 'doc' on a ship. The commanding officer said to me, 'If you apply yourself really well, there's potential for you to become the best student.' I was motivated to concentrate on academic study but torn between trepidation about failing and a keen sense of wanting to live life to the full. I talked with my roommates about our aspirations. I didn't want to go out at night, despite being allowed to. We were 17 and 18 in the era when no ID was needed in the pubs and it was almost summer.

The subjects covered were intense: anatomy and physiology, storekeeping, first aid, pharmacy, diagnostics, medical and surgical procedures and interventions, natural disasters and medical administration and nuclear and chemical attack. By the end of day two I was thinking, 'Oh my God, how am I going to get through this?' Medical administration referred to all the forms medical personnel have to fill in: for biopsies, drugs, requests from surgeons for second opinions and everything in between. They gave us a huge bible full of forms that we had to know inside out within six months. It was my first time learning by rote.

Anatomy was key. Because we would often be working solo in remote locations, we had to learn to diagnose very quickly what was wrong with an individual; we had to be doctor, surgeon and nurse all in one. I had to concentrate hard, using maths again. Suddenly it was logarithms, chemical symbols and algorithms. For post mortems, they sent us down to Haslar morgue to practise on dead bodies. We learnt to put in a chest drain to reinflate a lung. We'd view an intracranial viral illness in the spine diagnosed from a trauma in the head and drill a hole in the head to relieve the pressure. Nothing was viewed as too advanced but I felt totally out of my depth. I couldn't talk to my family and friends about these things. It helped to talk to my mates Pickering and Bostock instead. But, though nervous, I felt happy immersed in my studies and started to flourish as I applied myself in a way I never had before. Basic training had been easy after my upbringing, but this work took every ounce of my brain power.

In pharmacy we learnt every drug from morphine to barbiturates, barbitones and ointments. We also learnt how to make ointments from scratch so that, in a crisis situation, we knew what we could make use of. We learnt each chemical name, trade name, contraindication and dosage, every treatment that went with each diagnosis. When it came to dealing with real-life medical stuff, the navy expected absolute self-sufficiency. Civilian doctors often made terrible first aiders because they had limited hands-on practical experience. A naval first aider had to be nothing short of brilliant. Not only did you have to look at a blast or gunshot wound or disease, you had to run the intubation and do everything else that was required. For pathology we learnt to take a sample from someone by swabbing a lesion and then to do the follow-up. Many years later, these high-stakes, under-pressure skills would prove indispensable in Belfast and other conflict areas, and also when I was assessing ballistic and blast wounds during BBC journalist investigations. I was immeasurably grateful to have received such training.

A significant examination on all that term's content came all too quickly. This was a make-or-break test and the standards were extremely high. I focused on learning every procedure time and time again, but after three months I suffered a major setback: I failed pharmacy and occupational health and hygiene; the pass mark was 85 per cent. I was summoned to the training officer for a sobering 'little chat'. 'Loughran, it's not looking good. You've failed two subjects out of six. We have to back-class you. You're very close but you're going no further forward if you don't pass all six. I'm afraid we'll have to discharge you from the navy. Your tests show you can do the other subjects, so pull your socks up.' It was a necessary kick in the pants. The other guys were down at the pub; it got me thinking that maybe I wasn't good enough. My dad certainly thought so: 'You'll be a bin man,' he said when I rang. Mum told me to stick at it.

At the NAAFI I heard that Jeff had joined the Royal Fleet Auxiliary, which provides logistical and operational support to the Royal Navy and Royal Marines, and resolved to keep at it and work my arse off. By that stage of the course, everyone got their own cabins. I made notes on everything and sat at my desk all night, every night, until my final exams.

Our final test was in the pathology lab and morgue. I liked the lab. The size of a football pitch, located under the hospital, it had medical records on everything and displayed, in jars, a crazy assortment of pickled body parts showing gunshot wounds or strange abnormalities.

It was easy to fail an autopsy – one accidental scalpel nick of the intestines and you'd activate a truly dreadful smell. I put the headlamp on, explaining what I was doing before cutting the chest open. I could see the difference between the lungs: one had collapsed and it was this I had to diagnose. Using everything we'd learnt from anatomy and physiology lessons, I navigated my way around the body's interior, then dissected the lungs and named certain parts of the trachea.

My family didn't show for the passing out parade marking the end of my intense medical training. To achieve over 95 per cent in my exams, at the age of 19 when, really, I was destined for prison, filled me with pride. It was a huge honour to get this far, to have your name called out and the officer pin a medic badge on your uniform and publicly announce your achievements. My parents had witnessed my sister's and brother's special moments but, despite knowing the date of my parade, they missed it – and the surprise of my being awarded a prize for the student who developed the most during training.

Saying goodbye to my new-found friends was difficult as we'd formed such a bond over the 12 months spent at Haslar. Though relieved to have passed, I knew that I still hadn't qualified and to do this I had another year's worth of training in every medical category possible – surgery, orthopaedics, medical diseases, basic dentistry.

***

RNH Stonehouse in Plymouth, where I arrived in January 1982, was a very old hospital. It was a culture shock coming from a brand-new block to an eighteenth-century building with 30 patients to a ward – and dealing with the cockroaches that riddled the place. But somehow the medical staff who trained there created a brotherhood, and most still meet at an annual reunion.

After I'd completed three months of medical training, I was allowed to move out of the hospital quarters and was invited to share a house with three other medics, Gary Wright, Mick McMenemy and Mick Walsh, but in April 1982 the Argentinians decided to invade the Falklands and all three lads were drafted to sail away as part of the Navy & Royal Marines South Atlantic task force. This left me in a real jam as I'd taken on a lease with the others and had no one to help pay the bills. To add to my woes, I found out that they hadn't paid the milkman for months. This was a problem I could do without as my studies were getting longer and harder. The stakes couldn't have been higher: pass and I'd set myself up for a great career in the navy; fail and I'd be back on the streets of Liverpool facing a very uncertain future.

During this time, I started dating a beautiful naval nurse named Pauline and began to find my feet. I was almost 21 and had turned my life around. I was studying hard and desperate for a chance to prove myself, but the opportunities of going away to sea were scarce. It seemed like the navy was keen to keep all the medics back at navy establishments or the two naval hospitals. Although Pauline and I bought a house and moved in together, I felt myself in the same old routine: cycle to work for a day shift or very long night shift and then back home again. (Buying the house taught me a valuable life lesson. We needed £2000 to put down on a £21,000 mortgage and I had to ask my father for the money. Mum decided the request would come better from her but she called me back a few days later with a flat no from Dad. Since that day I have never requested money from anyone else. I procured the money from a French bank with an excruciatingly high interest rate but honoured every payment.)

Then one day I was summoned to the admin office and told that they were short of medics for HMS *Galatea*. The petty officer had hardly got his words out when I said a resounding, *'Yes*, you beauty.' *Galatea*, the 'Black Pig' as it was known in the navy, was a Leander class frigate tasked with checking for enemy submarines, underwater mines and other threats. With seven other ships, it was bound for the Mediterranean on a joint defence exercise with Italian, Greek and American warships. This was my first time at sea. As I walked up the gangplank with a swagger and a navy kitbag over my arm, I was the size of an ant compared with the enormous deck and pristine ship. The guns dwarfed me.

Eric Bachelor, the ship's senior medic, became my mentor. Thanks to his 1.9-metre height, you could always see him heading towards you in the ship's corridors, walking with a bent neck and arched back. Now I was working in the role for which I was trained, ready to spring into action at a moment's notice, diagnosing everything from STDs to foot rot.

It was traditionally a horrendously rough journey passing through the Bay of Biscay, where ships didn't bob or turn but corkscrewed in the water, but I didn't get sick once. It must have been the mariner genes running through my blood. As we sailed south, life onboard was never dull: we did man overboard exercises, fired weapons at floating targets and conducted manoeuvres with NATO forces, and we had a lot of fun.

As 2 March approached, it was looking as though my twenty-first birthday would be spent sailing into Venice, which I'd always wanted to visit. That morning we choppered into La Spezia, halfway between Genoa and Pisa, to drop an unwell helicopter pilot at a medical centre. I'd taken a look at the abscess in his tooth and realised we couldn't drain it on the ship; the tooth would have to come out under general anaesthetic. When the dentist in La Spezia emerged with a big cigarette hanging from the corner of his mouth, and I spotted a filthy farmyard cat sitting on the sterile dental tray, I said, 'We're out of here', and called in another flight to transport us both to another hospital.

A few days later we finally arrived in Venice and it was on with the business of celebrating my birthday, which the guys on board decided was to be spent in fancy dress so that the line-up on the flight deck for the departing salute included one of the lads dressed as a vicar, with little round glasses and clutching a copy of the Gideon Bible – 'Bless you, my son.' By 10 a.m. we were drinking beers in a gondola. As we passed by the Rialto Bridge, my mates dared me to jump off the bridge in my undies, into what I discovered was very smelly water, then took my clothes so that I was forced to wander around St Mark's Square in torrential rain, until someone called the police. When I found my mates, we carried on drinking, dropping the glass steins all over the floor of the outdoor pub. On the way back to the ship the lads all complained of sore feet. Looking more closely, with my drunkenly blurred vision, I could see that their feet were slashed from the broken steins and so spent the next five hours sobering up, picking out all the shards of glass and stitching up everyone's wounds. I'm sure there will still be some men wandering the earth with haphazardly stitched feet.

Back in Plymouth, it was lovely to see Pauline again and to settle into our new home, a very old and very small fisherman's cottage in Plympton, but now I'd had a taste for adventure and yearned for the next challenge. However, I settled back into my medical career at Stonehouse, a time I look back on with great fondness. I was working hard, but with the seriousness came some dark humour. One night, my best mate, John Roberts, decided to play a trick on a young naval nurse who had conducted the last offices on an elderly patient who had died. At the old, dark and creepy morgue John wrapped a medic mate from another ward in a hospital sheet, tying his big toes together as if he'd died, then inserted him into the fridge lying face up. The 'body' was instructed to start groaning the moment the nurse opened the door. What John and our mate Jim Tunnicliffe didn't know was that I'd also wrapped up a mate and positioned him above John's friend in the fridge. As the nurse approached, I heard John's mate in the fridge muttering, 'Bloody hell, I hope they get here soon. I'm fucking freezing.' At that point my mate above him couldn't resist responding with, 'You think you're cold. I've been in here for days.' There was much banging and shouting from the fridge, a completely blank look from John and the nurse took off like a horse chasing a carrot in a sandstorm and couldn't be found for hours.

***

My brother Jeff had lost his athleticism and, like most people in Liverpool in those days, smoked and drank a fair bit. I was thrilled to hear that he was heading to Oakhampton on the northern edge of Dartmoor, not far from Plymouth, for his basic training, and we'd be reunited for a few months. When we met, though, he was sitting in a room with a one-bar electric heater, trying to combat the freezing conditions. I felt really sorry for him. He'd been kicked out of art college for growing dope and selling it to the students. Dad had given him an ultimatum: get a job, move away or be thrown out – your choice. We spent many a night in Oakhampton before he was posted off to his first ship, HMS *Arrow*, and managed a cracking New Year at one of my local pubs in Saltash Passage.

We had no money and could only afford one beer. I told Jeff that we'd wait for 9 p.m., when everyone was drunk, and I'd lift up the lid on the small piano in the bar and away we'd go. 'But you can't play the piano,' said Jeff. 'Yeah, but they'll be drunk ...' I started singing Ray Charles' 'Mess Around', which I followed up with 'I've Got a Woman'. The place kicked off and the beers were filling the top of the piano. Jeff picked up two spoons and began playing a cool rhythm. We fell out of there at 3 a.m., totally smashed, cashed up and with four bookings for weddings and birthday parties.

On another occasion we'd spent the best part of a morning drinking Guinness and schnapps and around lunchtime I headed home to sleep it off before starting a night shift at 6 p.m. It was NTR – nothing to report – until approximately 11.30 p.m., when I heard my brother singing at the top of his voice, completely under the influence of a day's drinking with his navy mates. When he asked, 'Any chance I can crash here?', I spotted an empty bed in the side cabin reserved for special observation cases such as dive injuries like the bends. I threw Jeff a set of pale blue hospital pyjamas and he pulled the curtains around him and slipped into a deep drunken slumber.

The following morning, I was chasing my tail a bit, as we had to get all 25 patients up, cleaned and seated outside their beds ready for daily observations and breakfast. I completely forgot that Jeff was still snoring his head off in the side cabin when the senior surgeon commander entered the ward to start his medical rounds. Dave Owen, my night shift medic buddy, came to my rescue and filled out a chart at the end of Jeff's bed, giving him the name Leading Seaman Hugh Janus. As the surgeon commander got closer with his posse of junior doctors and nurses, I could see Jeff stirring and he didn't look good: his hair all matted with booze, saliva dribbling down his chin and pyjamas. Little did I realise that Dave had written on Jeff's notes, 'Diving Accident – severe case of the bends – inability to have any control of speech or movement of the body, to be transferred to the navy dive school to enter recompression.' The commander took one look at my brother and said, 'Ladies and gentleman, this is indeed a rare opportunity to study a patient and a medical phenomenon you don't see every day.'

Dave read out my brother's medical notes to the commander rather loudly to ensure that Jeff knew the scam. The commander shouted back, 'Dear God, you don't have to shout. I'm not deaf.' My brother then looked at Dave and the commander, pointing to his ears, and wrote on a piece of paper, 'I can't hear you.' The commander apologised in writing, then ushered the medical team out to let my brother rest a little more. The last thing I saw, through a crack between the curtains of another bed, was my brother, in his blue hospital pyjamas, clutching his clothes and heading for the fire escape.

Jeff went off to the Falklands and it was on the way back, in

Florida, that he got extremely drunk, ended up in a big fight with a couple of sailors and was sent back to Woolwich in London where, as he put it, 'he was placed on an alcoholics' basket weaving course', i.e. major detox. It was while he was at this clinic that he met Sue Medway, his future wife and best mate for life. He always believed that something good comes out of a shitty situation, and he was right.

***

I was restless and knew it was time for me to move on, but I really didn't know what to do. Then I got talking to John Roberts, who was now working in the medical centre of Stonehouse Barracks, home to 3 Commando Brigade, Royal Marines. He told me of the time he spent away and what he got up to and I knew this would be right up my alley. I pushed to secure a move to the barracks, the oldest in England. My persistence paid off and I joined the team.

One of the casualties of attachments to the commando world can be personal relationships and sadly mine was no exception. I loved Pauline dearly and we went into buying a house with our eyes wide open, full of promise and the opportunity to stay together, but the long weeks and months away, my young age at 23 and the influence from the lads to go out drinking combined to pull us apart. It is something I deeply regret to this day. I let Pauline down badly, particularly as she ended another relationship to be with me and had made sacrifices. The experience did, though, perhaps make me respect others more, especially those who went out of their way to help me.

It was the dead of winter when Dave Poole called me up. 'Hi Scouse, I've put your name forward for the commando course because the Marines are desperate for commando medics.' Dave had been a senior commando medic for a long time and I'd worked with him at Stonehouse. (My specialised medical training, which was designed to allow me to treat anyone anytime and anywhere, meant I was sought after by the submarine and commando services.) But I had to earn a right to be a commando. Because, with no commitments, I was having a ball drinking and lording it up, I had a shot at convincing Dave that they should put me on the summer commando course, rather than the usual two months' training in winter, but he was unimpressed: 'Yeah, sure, I'll throw in a valet and a cocktail cabinet as well.' That Christmas I attempted to do a bit of training but in reality I ate, drank and was the ultimate party animal. I always woke, though, with a voice in my head, like one of Scrooge's visiting ghosts in *A Christmas Carol*: 'Beware the commando course ... pain ... suffering ... discomfort – failure.'

I had reason to be wary. I'd always considered myself fit and found physical exercise easy. I put that down to running away from police, rival gangs and the occasional headmaster's wife as a kid. The commando course was notoriously gruelling, both mentally and physically, and the cause of serious injuries, from bilateral knee dislocations and fractured ankles to trench foot. I would actually see much worse. One lad fell 6 metres from a rope climb with full kit on, sustaining such bad bilateral ankle fractures that he damaged all the nerves and blood supply to his feet. He was told to get up and keep marking time.

To have any chance of landing a spot on the pass-in test for the course, in December 1984, I had to go through a week of hard physical training, aptly named the beat-up. Most army soldiers and navy ranks had trained seriously for months before with large heavy weights placed in their backpacks and long extended runs over the cold bleak Dartmoor countryside, punctuated with 500 sit-ups and press-ups in blocks of 100. I, on the other hand, had built muscle mass and stamina by swimming huge distances – 3 kilometres per day – with swim floats and kick paddles. I also never had a driving licence or car but cycled and ran everywhere. It stood me in good stead. Even during the beat-up, the most physically fit men had peaked and were sustaining injuries. I took everything in my stride and remained fit throughout.

By the end of the week, I felt strong and committed but I still didn't know if I'd made the cut. The regimental sergeant major (RSM) gave us the news in an interesting way. 'The following names take two paces forward,' he barked. After what seemed like an eternity, the last name was read out and mine wasn't there. My heart sank to the floor. I was sure I'd done enough to get through. What was going to become of me now? The next order from the RSM came as a complete surprise: 'The names I've read out will report back to your units. Although you've tried your utmost to gain a slot on the commando course, you've fallen short. To those names I didn't read out, congratulations on taking the first step towards earning your green beret and being part of the commando brotherhood.'

The smile on my face was huge but I knew that the toughest times lay ahead. I elected not to share this news with my family for two reasons: (1) I hadn't passed anything yet, and (2) I thought they wouldn't have a clue as to what the commando world was all about. Little did I know that in 1987, when Prince Edward quit the same course, my father was allegedly showing off photos of me receiving my green beret and the Commando Medal and telling everyone, 'See, look at this. A woolly woofter royal can't pass the commando course but my lad did, so that makes him better than a royal.' I only heard of this after Dad died and it came as a pleasant shock.

***

Commando Training Centre (CTC) Lympstone had its own train station at Exmouth and in January 1985 I alighted to meet some really lean and mean-looking commandos. The fiercest of the lot was the drill sergeant, with his green beret, shiny cap badge, maple wood strip under one arm, huge thick moustache and highly polished black boots. Our tiny lockers and bed spaces in the dorms were the worst living quarters I'd encountered so far in terms of space and privacy. The instructors and surroundings were there to break us. Only a small percentage of trainees went on to be awarded the coveted green beret; those in charge expected resilience as the rest of us expect having air to breathe.

We were issued green fatigues and a green woolly cap comforter, nicknamed the Noddy hat, which folds and covers the top of your head. At the armoury we signed out a long SLR, a 9-millimetre pistol and a cleaning kit. Everything about the course was specially designed to screw you around mentally and physically. Within five minutes we were expected to strip the weapon and memorise every single part of it, then told to report to the infamous Bottom Field, which was synonymous with commando course training torture. The final test was 12 hours of physical beasting. There were several tasks to complete during this time, including kitten crawling on top of a taut rough hessian rope over a huge ice-cold water tank, climbing a 9-metre rope to ring a bell at the top as well as full on physical circuits on the Bottom Field that resulted in excessive vomiting, heat exhaustion and collapse.

I shared the pass-in test with all ranks and services, including navy pilots and air crew, whose job it was to shuttle and insert a number of commando units behind enemy lines. At one stage, I saw a military padre wandering around foaming at the mouth, trying to use his cross as a weapon (which we weren't allowed). It was like a scene from *Dad's Army* as he ran around shouting, 'Bang, bang, you're dead.'

After six hours, one guy next to me shouted 'I want out' and was promptly and unceremoniously thrown into the back of a 4-tonne military truck. At the eighth hour, my eyeballs were rolling and my mouth frothing, but I kept thinking, 'I can't let myself or my dad down.' The magical moment was when there were five of us left out of 60. I climbed the rope with tortured, blistered hands and rang the bell. The last part of the test was the icy tank where we had to tread water. The course officer yelled, 'Right, you little scrote bags, you've passed your final test if you exit the water with something that resembles a hard-on.' Surprisingly, even though my entire body had closed down and I couldn't feel my hands, all five of us rose to the occasion, so to speak. As I hosed my kit down and dried it off, I felt a warm glow: I'd made it. It was another step on my hard and long journey but I couldn't help feeling a tinge of sadness for all those who had failed.

I spent the weekend buying as much kit as I could – socks, boot polish and waterproof bags – because I knew that by Monday morning I'd be reporting back to CTC and hitting the ground running. On that first day, I noticed many of the guys were older than me and considerably more experienced in the field, but, like me, they'd been drafted onto the course. The following day we learnt every single weapon you can possibly think of, from handling an SLR to the standard L2 hand grenade. We learnt weapons theory and unarmed combat. We learnt to kill by choking. We learnt very quick and effective ways to break bones and how to silently kill with the commando dagger. We spent hours on the firing ranges ensuring we could fire a weapon from every conceivable position and angle with extreme accuracy.

Every aspect of the training got steadily harder, culminating in passing the various commando tests that were designed to keep pushing you to the maximum. You were always looking over your shoulder to see who else had quit. We had to hike 10 miles, as it was then – about 16 kilometres – carrying a 50-kilogram load and the objects were really difficult to manage, not just because of their weight but because they were bulky, like the general purpose machine gun or 'gimpy', as it's affectionately known. We'd often be stopped and questioned on different parts of the weapon. This wasn't just to see if you knew your stuff but also to play with your mind when you were fatigued.

The 6- and 9-mile marches were tough and it paid to line yourself up in the middle to the front of the squad as anyone at the rear would fall behind as soon as the pace increased. The 30-mile march was even tougher. We would be out in the field all week in Dartmoor, sometimes with nowhere to shelter, exposed to the harshness of the moors. Any sleep you could get was taken sitting down in the freezing cold with your poncho over your head. Our ponchos also doubled up as the tent sheet, secured to separate trees by a couple of bungy cords.

The injuries sustained during this particular challenge were considerable: stress fractures, a torn Achilles tendon, frostbite, frostnip, nails falling off, blurred vision and noticeable weight loss. They gave us rations for meals that, if ruined or eaten, were not replaced. The objective was to not be seen: we had to stay under the radar, escape and evade. I shared the first night in our poncho tent with a Scottish guy, who accidentally kicked over the food I had just finished cooking on my small fuel block stove. We were absolutely starving, and the prospect of being tasked again by the training team on an empty stomach did not appeal one bit. So I ripped up the rules and broke into a local farmhouse, stole some eggs and scavenged a couple of useful things like waterproof fertiliser bags and a small spade.

Only a few nights into the exercise I looked outside my tent sheet and saw that my companion had had enough: he'd stuck a tree branch in his weapon like a surrender flag and admitted defeat. I tried my best to encourage him, telling him to snap out of it and keep going, but at 3 a.m., with the training team watching from a surveillance point, he got into a warm truck and was spirited away. I was left on my own. They made me do 20 press-ups, strip my weapon and catch up to everyone else. I learnt a lesson: never leave a man behind. They told me I'd let him quit and that he was hallucinating due to the cold weather.

Back at the base we had to complete a Tarzan assault course on which there had been deaths in the past. There were tunnels to wriggle through and walls to be scaled, all within a certain time. There was also what was known as a smartie tube, a 30-metre underground tube that you had to enter headfirst, lying on your back, and then push yourself along with your heels and back, your weapon lying on your chest. With no light to guide us, it was extremely dark, claustrophobic, cold and wet and felt never-ending. Someone deliberately spilled cow's offal when we went through. I passed the first time so I was really pleased.

After completing my final commando test, I remember seeing the commanding officer of Lympstone walking up and down, stepping over bodies and reading out official numbers, then placing the green berets on our heads as we saluted him. Out of 30 of us, 20 passed this section of the course. He said to me, 'My team watched you all the way through the course. You have the commando spirit. There's a nice little surprise coming for you, Loughran.'

The Commando Medal was occasionally awarded to the best recruit on the course. When my name was read out to receive it, I was astonished. The training team had been observing me throughout the entire course and were unanimous in their decision. The award brought me a flurry of congratulations from high-ranking officers in the Royal Navy and Royal Marine Commando world.

CHAPTER 6
COLD AND HARD

'Hey Scouse, well done on your award. See, I told you you'd do well.'
It was Dave Poole again, calling from Commando headquarters at
Hamoaze House, Plymouth. Then he asked me if I was sitting down
and told me that my next mission, should I choose to accept it,
was to join an elite Special Forces Commando Unit, the Mountain
& Arctic Warfare Cadre (M&AW), which had achieved legendary
status after the Falklands War. The M&AW had begun in the 1950s
as the Royal Marine Cliff Assault Wing, set up to train marines in
cliff assaults and rock climbing techniques. (It would be renamed
the Mountain Leader Training Cadre in the early 1990s.)

Although I wasn't aware of all the cadre's achievements, I knew
straight away that I would be joining to give medical support to a
very tight band of brothers. In September 1986 I walked through the
gates of Stonehouse Barracks, an old Napoleonic fort, to be greeted
by a small but hard-looking man, Warrant Officer Des Wassall.
(This incredible man, who died in 2016 at the age of 67, was a Royal
Marine and Falklands veteran who received the Military Medal and
an MBE.) 'You must be our new doc,' he said, staring me right in
the eyes. 'Yes sir,' came my swift reply. 'Well, you'd better be better
than the last one.'

I signed out all my stores, climbing gear, ice axes, crampons, ropes and a thing that looked like a small L-shaped metal plate. Later I found out it was aptly named the dead man, used to stop you falling into a crevasse. I was fitted for my first pair of skis, which looked suspiciously like two wooden planks painted white. With them went an ugly pair of leather boots with a square toe cap that looked not unlike the shitty old football boots Dad had once bought me. I was issued with a 9-millimetre pistol, submachine gun and an M16 with an underslung grenade launcher.

I was to be with the Mountain Leader (ML2s) course. My role was to supply medical cover or rope access assistance to anyone requiring immediate medical help, but the more I worked with the ML team, the more I immersed myself in all the challenges they faced. I had the great fortune of being supported by Dave Poole, who was the lead commando medic for the team, and Des Wassall. Dave had handpicked me for this role because the cadre had lost faith and confidence in the previous medic. They needed someone who could fit in immediately and last the distance and keep pace. I was working with 12 super-fit and resourceful Marines and soldiers drawn from various Royal Marine Units, Dutch Special Forces and UK and Australian SAS. We bonded to such a degree that we rolled through the nine months really well, at times as if our lives depended on it.

The course began at Sennen Cove in Cornwall, which offered myriad challenging climbing walls. Arriving at the cove after an 8-kilometre run, we sprinted to the top of the cliff and there before me was a wide and deep cavern dropping dramatically to a huge granite ledge jutting out over the rough and unpredictable English Channel. Bored with sitting at the top of the climbs, I pulled out my kit and started to gingerly descend the 60-metre cliff face through the aptly named Grip Tight Gully. It was dark, wet and extremely slippery due to the lack of sunlight and crashing waves pummelling the rock face. I reached the bottom of the cavern and then had to ascend. Apart from scaling the electric pylon in Liverpool, and the outside of my house if I'd been locked out, I'd never done any real climbing. As I stared up at the route my jaw dropped. My climbing partner, 'Ginge' Forrester, a tough Glaswegian, laughed. 'You've got this. Whatever you do, don't look down and don't fart or shit your pants, especially if I'm climbing below you.'

I found the climb hard but I loved the thrill of exposure, of being on a vertical rock face with nothing but the wild ocean before me. When I reached the top, Ginge said, without missing a beat, 'You've just done the easy bit. Wait until we start to climb in big boots with kit weapons and webbing. Oh, and throw in the night climb and we'll review this again.' My heart sank: somehow even though I'd completed my first climb I realised I'd failed the first test: 'Don't be smug or heady, remain humble and move through each task quietly and with confidence.' This became a huge life lesson for me.

After a full day's climbing, I was encouraged to join the 2s course and run the 10 kilometres back along the beach, which included a lot of sand dune sprints and firemen's carries. That night I had to give a lecture on gunshot wounds. I opened by saying that even though I was relatively young, I'd spent a great deal of time in a number of high-risk accident and emergency areas and got blooded, so to speak, by analysing and tending to gangland gunshot wounds and knife attacks. When I was training, the naval hospitals were rammed full of medics and there was little, if any, chance to practise such vital lifesaving skills as intubation, finding a vessel or artery and clipping it off or finessing the art of cannulation. A training mannequin or anatomical head just didn't feel the same. So the navy reached out to a number of public hospitals whose accident and emergency bays were littered with casualties who looked like they'd come from straight off a battlefield. The only difference was the lack of uniform and the stench of alcohol and vomit. I'd been seconded to Sheffield's Royal Hallamshire Hospital, Southampton General and the Royal Hospital in London's Whitechapel.

After experiencing the chaotic and arduous phase one, it was time to move on to the second phase, which involved climbing for longer and harder, and Llanwrst in Wales had this kind of landscape in abundance. Having grown up in Liverpool, I'd often visited North Wales and Llandudno but nothing prepared me for the beauty of the deep lush valleys and long steep roads. Wales was a tough gig: the climbing was brutal and the weather was atrocious, wet, cold and miserable. But the days came and went and before we knew it we were about to embark on the survival phase of the training. It was set in a very beautiful but remote island of Islay, positioned in the weather-beaten part of Scotland's Outer Hebrides. Not long after that, the 2s course entered into a tactical ops phase back in Stonehouse Barracks, using Dartmoor as a location for tactics such as sniper training and close target recce.

***

We were heading into Christmas and I still had two important courses to deal with before the holiday break. To be embedded in the cadre I had to be ski and ice climb fit but I didn't have a winter's experience under my belt, so Des signed me and three Dutch Special Forces guys up to a novice ski course. It was run in Rjukan, Norway, which was grey and bleak and apparently had the highest rainfall in the world. It was also dark for the most days in a year. On the final day we were taught telemarking, which requires you to 'squat' on the skis as you descend. With our personal kits packed in bergens (or rucksacks) and carrying an M16 and loaded magazines – plus, in my case, the team's 55-kilogram medical kit – we started traversing the deep snowline to the top of the mountain. For most of the morning I spent more time buried in the snowline than on top.

The course came to an end and we'd passed. The next challenge was mountain training in Scotland. This was harsh, designed to teach the MLs how to take large groups of marines or soldiers up a mountain and onto a military objective. Then, in January 1986, came another stint in Norway for Arctic survival training. As we stepped off the plane at Oslo we estimated that it was approximately minus 10 degrees at the airport and dropping to minus 20 with the wind chill factor.

The journey to our destination of Sjoa really moved me; I was in awe of my new white blanketed surroundings and found myself singing the Beatles classic 'Norwegian Wood' as we moved deeper and deeper into the remote Arctic wastes. But such romantic thoughts would soon be wiped out.

Since I'd been with the ML2s course more or less all the way through, it was recommended that I join them in the field. This was no mean feat, as it meant we'd leave Sjoa on Monday and be back on Friday afternoon, that's if you'd survived white outs, wind chill, minus 40 degree temperatures and the occasional avalanche. We were dropped by helicopter into a dangerously isolated territory where one slip could end up in permanent disability or death. After the first few days, we managed to establish some sort of order, and apart from the occasional blister and some frostnip, everyone remained in good health. At the end of every week, the course would be extracted at Friday lunchtime and enjoyed a long hot shower and the chance to feel human again.

After many weeks the day arrived, in March 1986, for the ML2s course winter pass-out test, which involved a 10-day 200-kilometre Arctic field test. Like the survival course in Islay, this was a straight pass or fail, but to make matters worse, if you failed you had to start the past seven months of training all over again. By now I had formed an incredible bond with all the course members and pleaded with Dave Poole and the M&AW instructional team to enter the field with the 2s course. I'd be with one specific group: Gordon Messenger, Bo Bomeister, Pat O'Flynn and Billy Baxter. I knew I had to be on my A game, since nothing or no one was going to stand in the way of this ace team passing the course. I now realise that the entire course trusted me and valued me both as a skilled medic and important team member. It was an honour I feel to this day. I think, too, they liked the fact I could not only carry my own kit and weapon but a huge med pack as well: I was literally a mobile doctor and pharmacy.

The days passed by, bringing task after task, but the memory of one night still haunts me. We were traversing a steep and remote mountain range in a wind that was attacking our extremities from all directions. The temperature by now had dropped to minus 35 degrees. The snow at this level was compacted and riddled with sastrugi, raised snake-like icy patterns on the snowline that can snap a ski or your ankle. Digging my metal ski edges into the ice on the mountain, I looked down at my skis and wondered why they were moving and yet we were static. Had it not been for Billy's quick thinking in clipping onto my harness and banging an ice screw into the mountain, I would have tumbled more than 900 metres to my death. I didn't realise I was in the advanced stages of exhaustion and hypothermia, and everything was starting to appear as one blurred blue colour. I'd sweated so much over the past few hours that the perspiration had turned to ice on my skin and the wind chill was biting into my body. Billy reached for his thermos flask and made me guzzle down a litre of hot sweet tea.

After being caught in a whiteout that night, I woke up at 0200 and noticed the light from the candle inside the snow cave dimming. Some of the other men were also running out of candles. It was important to keep these burning as an indicator that oxygen was present. I decided to invert my metal mess tin and slice a candle with my extremely sharp knife. But I was so exhausted that the blade slipped and cut through my left index finger, severing tendon and bone. The blood immediately spurted across the cave and a dozy Billy woke up to see blood pumping all over his sleeping bag. Immediately and instinctively, I clenched my fist and the bleeding slowed down a little. I felt my heart racing, my mouth went dry and a huge wave of nausea passed over me. I went into shock, the pain was so intense.

I pulled a tourniquet from my med kit and got Billy to apply it to the base of my finger and the bleeding stopped immediately. But I couldn't leave the tourniquet on forever or I'd lose my finger. 'Billy,' I said, 'it's your lucky day. You're about to get a crash course in stitching up a really messy wound.' Billy smiled and said in his thick Irish accent, 'Bring it on, you fucking beauty.' Under instruction, he drew up 20 millilitres of lignocaine, a local anaesthetic and numbing agent, and injected it into the base of my finger and top of my hand. I then showed Billy how to use the forceps and how to hold the needle and line. He delivered 15 perfectly positioned stitches, the traces of which I can still see today.

Three days after we'd been caught in the whiteout, two choppers landed at our position and a number of soldiers dressed in Russian Arctic uniforms got out and stormed our position. What I didn't realise was that this was actually 42 Commando's fiercely brutal recce team and this was the start of the R2I (Resistance 2 Interrogation phase). We were all stripped naked and left outside with dogs barking and patrolling around us, then taken inside and, for at least 12 hours, forced into impossible positions that made our bodies hurt like you wouldn't believe. I saw no one, was given nothing and was told to stay quiet or face elimination from the team and the exercise. At one stage I could feel a terrible throb in my finger, which by now was going numb with the pain and the cold. Later in my life, this experience would help me to cope when I had to deal with questioning, and potential kidnap, by the Taliban.

Then came the interrogation, sitting blindfolded on a very small chair, then having the hood removed and a bucket of ice-cold water thrown straight in my face, and a pulsing light flashed into my eyes. I stared at a man dressed in a full Cossack outfit, his face centimetres away from mine, screaming in Russian. To his right sat an older woman reading a book and smoking a cigarette. Between them they hammered me with questions, employing a good cop/bad cop routine. A steady flow of relentless questioning followed, along with demeaning inspections of my naked body.

***

The euphoria I felt getting through this tricky challenge was short-lived. I was two minutes into a conversation with my new girlfriend, Sue, from the main phone at Sjoa, when she announced that she was ending our relationship and had gone back to her previous boyfriend. I was devastated: I was about to invite her to come and live with me in Plymouth. This incident had a profound effect on me. For a long time, I lost faith in serious relationships for fear of rejection, which in hindsight was a link to my father's treatment of me as a young boy. I would spend years on my own just hanging out with the lads, having fun and drifting in and out of relationships. I never blamed Sue, though; we were both very young.

With the ML2s course over, June 1986 brought the annual trip to Lauterbrunnen in Switzerland, known as Exercise Ice Flip, during which we tackled higher grade ice climbs on such surrounding mountains as the Mönch, the Jungfrau and infamous Eiger. It all felt like a holiday and was a complete distraction from my doubts about staying in the commandos, and the navy for that matter, as I couldn't see a break from the constant deployments throughout the year.

When we returned to Plymouth, I marched into the boss's office to tell him that I was planning to leave and would be gone within 12 months. He dropped his pen and stared at me. 'Are you sure this is what you want?' I assured him it was and we chatted for an hour and then he informed me that he would arrange for me to join one of the commando units as they needed another doc to join them for their next nine-month operational phase. Two weeks later I received my papers informing me I was joining Bickleigh-based 42 Commando Unit. I had been joined at the hip with the entire team of the M&AW Cadre, and I've never met a more loyal, funnier and crazier bunch of delinquents in all my life. Among them was my mad partner in fun, Jim Giles, who had been a huge support. It was hard to say goodbye to the team but I knew I needed another challenge.

CHAPTER 7
BELFAST AND BEYOND

AFTER SPENDING A brilliant time trekking around the Lake District, I reported back to Bickleigh and joined L Company, considered the best out of all 42 Commando. As we lined up on the parade square, I felt a sense of relief that I was finishing an action-packed career which had started at the age of 18. It turned out, however, that I'd been highly recommended for a winter deployment to Norway that would go as far north in the Arctic Circle as possible. I'd been promised January to March to sort out my shit, hand in my kit and then go on a pre-release from service course, but, in the words of the warrant officer, 'Your arse now belongs to me and Her Majesty the Queen and if our glorious commander-in-chief wants your arse in the field, then her wish is my command. Besides that, we have a full-strength commando team, apart from a medic who I fear the lads will harm as they can't stand him.' And with that my chance of getting out early vanished and I had to endure two months of frozen hell before I could even think of applying for immediate release.

It was indeed a tough gig and as the last day came we were glad to be leaving. But before we boarded our flight back to the UK, we learnt we'd be going on two weeks' leave, and then reporting back at Bickleigh for our pre-Northern Ireland training before we deployed into Belfast.

We arrived in Belfast on 9 June 1989 and tried to settle as best we could. We were as nervous as hell. It was the twentieth anniversary of British troops being in Northern Ireland and we were all expecting a busy time. Our unit was there to maintain control of the area as sectarian fighting was still at an all-time high and for the IRA the chance to take out a Royal Marine Commando Unit and 3 PARA attachment would be seen as an ultimate achievement.

At the age of 28 I could cope with most things but reality bit when one of our own was shot and killed. It happened in one of the regular IRA haunts. Things were eerily quiet that night. Virtually no one was out on the streets, which is always an ominous sign and an indicator that an attack is imminent. The words everyone dreaded came over the radio, 'Contact wait out', which meant someone was firing directly onto our position. A suspect vehicle, heavily loaded down at the back, which indicated a bomb, tore past our position to the sound of automatic gunfire.

I heard what sounded like a mosquito moving around my head, but was in fact bullets flying by. At this point I was seeking as much hard cover as possible and then I heard a hard thud and realised that someone to my left had been hit, though in the chaos I didn't know who. The bullets continued to fly in the direction of the suspect vehicle and then the call came out that one of our team was injured. The patrol formed an overall protective arc of cover around our fallen man.

I conducted a primary survey – a quick medical assessment of the head, throat and chest. I could feel something sticky and moist, which I first thought was sweat and rain. The tell-tale sign that it was blood was the distinct metallic taste I had in my mouth after licking my finger. We had to get out of there fast. When I pulled his head back and opened up his airway, I was shocked to see a torrent of bubbling oxygenated blood pouring down his throat and running into his lungs: he was drowning in his own blood. I quickly intubated him by guiding the tube through the blood and into his trachea. I cut his body armour off and sliced open both sleeves of his combat smock. In the darkness I tried desperately to find a vein: he'd lost so much blood. I managed to get one cannula in and connected the fluid bag, which gave him urgently needed fluids and painkillers. There was no improvement, just a faint thready pulse. My medic colleague Monty got another cannula in and we then piggy-backed both lines and at one stage were standing on the fluid bags to increase his blood volume. All the while we were still coming under fire from a position no one could trace.

Only then did I recognise 18-year-old Ian Gilbert (Gilly). I knew him well. I'd spent two months of a brutal winter on an exercise with him. Despite checking his body, we couldn't find a bullet hole, just a scratch on his forehead. We raced to Musgrave Hospital in the armoured ambulance and it was at this stage that I noticed a 2-centimetre mushroom-shaped mark on the back of his ear. That, we would later discover, was the exit hole. I remember Monty and I performing CPR on Gilly until we got him on the theatre trolley. But then a doctor whispered in my ear, 'He's gone, lad. You've done your best. And if he'd survived he'd have lived his life as a complete vegetable.'

An officer I knew had mistakenly shot Gilly in the head, close to where we were standing. This experience hardened me but also affected me deeply. I could feel the incident drifting constantly in and out of my mind. Certain objects and odours would take me right back to the night of the shooting. To this day I get flashbacks when I smell diesel; it had been sloshing around the gutter. This, of course, was post-traumatic stress disorder, PTSD, but I had no idea I was experiencing it. I'd dealt with death before, but this was different. At that time PTSD wasn't even considered a problem in the military but I remember hardened Marines telling me that they certainly had it after the Falklands, though the treatment then was to get pissed and go on leave. As I explain later, families were sent an explanatory letter, but counselling was never thought of, let alone offered. On many occasions some of the senior non-commissioned officers said to young recruits straight after a traumatic event, 'Well, if you can't stand the sights, then don't put on the uniform.' I hope those NCOs can look at all the homeless veterans lining the pavements and apologise to them for their lack of leadership in tackling this dreadful situation for which so much can now be done.

At the halfway mark of this tour, I was scheduled for some R & R, which meant I would be leaving Belfast for a week. I'd chosen to spend it in Manchester with Tracie, my girlfriend from Plymouth. I'd known her for a long time but we'd only dated for a few years. As my team boarded the aircraft for the short flight, I felt an incredibly peaceful feeling wash over me. For the previous three months I'd slept in my uniform, body armour and boots and was always on edge. On the way to a beautiful cottage on the edge of the Lake District that had been lent to us, Tracie said she had a sneaking suspicion she was pregnant but wanted me to be there when she found out. No sooner had we arrived in the cottage than she did the test and sure enough it was positive. I was both shocked and ecstatic, but we agreed that we wouldn't share the news with anyone until I got home in November, as we were planning to get married that month.

Back in Belfast it was as if I'd never left. Despite the fact that I was going to be a dad, I volunteered for everything and anything; the harder the operational task the better. I'd had plenty of time on my break to think about how I'd like to be remembered after leaving the world's best commando force and how I could honour the lives and heroism of those who had fallen. The answer was by taking risks and throwing myself into danger. Our time in Belfast had many highs and lows, too many to mention, but we did record a response to 33 separate incidents of attack and considered the tour a success.

When we arrived back at Plymouth at the end of October 1989 we were told to give our loved ones a letter that stated: 'Your son/ husband has just completed a tour of Belfast, where he may have been involved in a shooting, bombing or received unwanted verbal and physical abuse. Please note that he might not be able to sleep, will go to sleep with all his clothes on, and flinch and head for the nearest brick wall if a car backfires or if he experiences any loud bangs.' That note never made it to Tracie. I simply mislaid it and then completely forgot about it. In truth, there was good reason to issue such a letter. The world in which we'd just been submerged was completely alien to most people and it was next to impossible for those left at home to understand the nightmares, mood changes and emotional withdrawals that so often haunt those in the military.

In November 1990 I would receive an unexpected call from the Ministry of Defence informing me I had been awarded a GOC (General Officer Commanding) Commendation for outstanding skill and cool professionalism during my work in Northern Ireland, and in particular for the way I responded to the many shootings and attacks throughout the tour. I still feel, though, that the honour I received belonged to my colleague Monty and our entire unit and in particular to the many, like Gilly, who never came home.

***

After Belfast, I was already certain that I needed to go: I was hungry for fresh challenges and there were no more rungs for me on the promotional ladder. I could see many Marines and naval personnel who, like me, had joined up at 18, but were now close to 40. I realised that I, too, could end up stuck in the military groove and it wasn't something I wanted. One CO tried to persuade me to stay and have a crack at joining the Special Boat Service but although the chance to join such an elite outfit excited me, I knew I'd become institutionalised and that if I didn't leave now I'd end up in Defence until I retired.

I was also about to embark on something that neither the navy nor the commandos would have any influence on: becoming a husband and a father. On 25 November 1989, during a quiet service in Plymouth, Tracie and I got married. All my family and best friends were in attendance but Dad. This time, there was no excuse offered; it was just accepted that he avoided any event where you had to socialise. Although I felt deflated and embarrassed that he wasn't there, I'd got used to being let down and I didn't let his absence spoil the day.

After a final goodbye drinks with the lads in Stonehouse Barracks, I headed home. For the first time in 10 years I didn't have to be anywhere and I didn't have to wear a uniform, which was strange but liberating. I soon, however, grew tired of the stillness around me and missed the commando world and the camaraderie with the lads. Tracie was working but I still hadn't found work and so was home alone most days in a four-bedroom house overlooking Dartmoor, where I'd spent many a dark, lonely and often sleepless night. It was a constant reminder of the life I'd left behind.

It wasn't until two weeks after I'd finished up that I received a call from Jim Tunnicliffe, a great friend of mine and an enormously caring and generous guy. Jim suggested we meet for a beer and he'd give me the lowdown on what life was like on the oil rigs. He could put my name forward for a stint as a medic, if I was interested. I jumped at the chance: I was keen to get away, try something new and get back into work. The money was incredible but it was two weeks on the rig and two weeks off, and since I'd be working for an employment agency I wasn't guaranteed work, and as I found out later you never got paid for the fortnight off. But it was a start.

On 17 January 1990, Tracie gave birth to our daughter Brianna at Derriford Hospital in Plymouth. I felt incredible pride and joy holding this tiny bundle in my arms, thinking to myself, *Oh my God, I'm a dad. Is this really real?* Along with the joy came an overwhelming wave of responsibility. Brianna was so helpless, completely dependent on Tracie and me. I left the hospital in the early hours of the morning and caught a taxi home. The emotion was suddenly all too much. I leant forward and planted a kiss on the driver's cheek and proclaimed, 'I'm a *dad*! Oh, my God, I'm a *dad*!' His response was, 'Nice, mate. Do you want me to go via another route into Marsh Mills roundabout? There's a shitload of traffic there ...'

It was an exciting time with a new baby and new challenges, but also scary as many people were being laid off work and the dole queue was getting bigger. I didn't want to wait around to be an unemployment statistic and so made preparations to join the rigs. I was now torn: I wanted to spend as much time as possible with my wife and Brianna but knew I had to get out of Plymouth to have any chance of securing a half-decent job and something I was trained for.

My introduction to life on the rigs was a one-day survival training course in the coastal town of Mablethorpe in north-east England. The main aim was to teach you sea survival and to test your nerve when placed in a helicopter escape tank. Having passed this, I headed back to Plymouth and some family time. The agency put me up for a night in a hotel before taking me to my first job on the huge Ninian Central oil and gas platform in the North Sea, off the coast of Scotland. My job was platform medic for two weeks, dealing with anything from amputation to removing metal splinters from the eyes of a welder who was grinding without goggles. The first injury I treated was a gaping gash on a guy's leg. It had been crushed and he had to be choppered off immediately to get treatment. My naval commando experience prepared me well for life on the rigs: being always first on the scene, facing often multiple injuries in extreme environments and remaining cool under pressure.

I stuck it out for 10 months as the agency sent me out to various jobs in the oil and gas industry. It was unpredictable work. I'd drive home after a job and often wait two weeks for a call. Sometimes a job would fall through at the last minute. I lost respect for many of those in charge: they were just cowboys, who knew nothing about the injuries the guys got on the job. One company I worked for would often cover up injuries and deaths and if they heard of anyone complaining, the pay chit at the end of their shift would be stamped NRB: not required back.

***

On one particular job, around June 1990, I'd no sooner landed on the rig than I received a call in the radio shack from Jeff telling me that Dad had just had a stroke and was in Walton Hospital in Liverpool. The oil rig manager was extremely supportive and booked me out on the last chopper flying between the rigs that afternoon. I hired a car from Aberdeen and drove south for five hours. I arrived at 2 a.m. and rushed onto the hospital ward, only to see an empty bed. Had I really not been in time to say goodbye to my dad? Then through the frosted glass of a door leading out onto the fire escape I saw a silver-haired man with a puff of smoke rising above his head. There sat Dad drawing on a Woodbine and looking up at me. 'What kept you?' I could easily have been done for murder. It appeared that he'd suffered a minor ischemic attack, a narrowing of the arteries to the brain. This was to be one of many before he suffered a massive stroke at 52. After 10 dreadful years of being institutionalised and at the mercy of the health care system and many greedy private nursing home operators, he died. Although she sometimes had to take three buses to get there, Mum continued to visit Dad even he when he continued to verbally abuse her. She made light of it, kept her head high and remained loyal to him until the end.

When I look back, I realise I really didn't know my dad nor he me, and I put this down to his hardly being there during my teenage years due to his many afternoons and evenings at the St Benet's Catholic Club. After I turned 18 and left, I returned to Liverpool only on special occasions. I enjoyed my time back home as Dad loved showing me off amid the safety of his drinking buddies at the club. I would watch him playing dominoes and getting jittery as the bell was about to be rung for last orders. On hearing this, Dad would amble up to the bar and in his massive hands would bring three half-pints of bitter back to the table, then consume them over the space of 30 minutes. I always dreaded the walk home as he'd stop to talk to stray dogs, cats and the occasional homeless person.

I raced to be at his deathbed in 2001. I remember walking into his room and seeing his piercing blue eyes fixed on the ceiling, with Mum, my sister Angela and Nancy the Irish matron near his bed. Nancy said to me in her broad brogue, 'Tony, we knew all your dad's little tricks. He could never get one over on us.' I said, 'Don't think so', and reaching under the table pulled out three cigarettes taped to its underside. I then pulled the head off a statue of Jesus by his bed and poured out another 10 cigarettes. As soon as I did this

Nancy said, 'You cheeky little shit, Brian. You played all of us for 10 years.' The last thing I remember was seeing my dad's beaming smile and then came his last gasp of air.

***

At the end of 1990, I received a phone call that changed my life. It was from Gavin Birkett, Senior Safety Adviser for the BBC. When the BBC had engaged the M&AW Cadre to film a sequence on flight, fright and fear for their science programme, *Tomorrow's World*, he had apparently taken a shine to me. There was a job going at the BBC in London to look after safety and security. It was perfect for someone with my skill set – high risk oriented, with diving and firearms experience.

I discussed the proposition with Tracie. We were living in Plymouth and Brianna was only a few months old, so making the nine-hour return trip from London to Plymouth each weekend wouldn't work. We would have to move to London. But I was desperate to leave the rigs and money was extremely tight: I had £20 left in my bank account, I couldn't afford petrol and I needed to support my family. I felt I had no option but to take the plunge. If I got the job I would have a two-year contract, security I couldn't pass up after the uncertainty of the agency work in oil and gas. It was another fortunate break in my life; I was going to try my damnedest to interview well.

CHAPTER 8
JOINING THE BBC

IN MID-JANUARY 1991 I headed up to London on the train the evening before my job interview with the BBC, wearing my best and only suit, and went to a blues bar on Edgware Road to meet my cousin, Nicky, for a drink. At the end of the night, I stumbled out, tripped over and landed with my face in the gutter, ripping my suit at the knees and vomiting. Nicky hauled me into a taxi and packed me off to my hotel.

I woke up at 9 a.m. I ducked briefly into a shop to see if a felt pen the colour of my suit would disguise the damage. Taking the underground train to the BBC television studios, stuffed in between commuters, only worsened my hangover. I felt like hell. I was late for the interview; the alcohol was oozing out of my pores. Bill Murdoch, a former army guy, kept asking me questions about tent eye (a medical condition where fumes build up in a tent or snow cave) and all I wanted to do was run out and spew. The job went to a woman with an impressive portfolio and I left London deflated, broke and feeling awful. Then Dave Walker rang to offer me the position. 'You were the most impressive candidate. We discovered the portfolio didn't belong to the woman who was offered the job. You were pissed, weren't you? We all put £5 on when you were going to vomit – that's why we kept asking you stupid questions.'

It was great to have a two-year contract but while I was waiting for the money to come through I couldn't afford a train ticket to get to work. I had to jump the turnstiles for about a month but managed to escape the train inspector and deep embarrassment.

Being out in the field meant I worked on some amazing projects, but the long hours put a huge strain on my marriage. In addition to this, I was spending every spare weekend studying for the occupational safety qualification I needed. I was so dedicated to making my job a success that one winter, when south-east London was caught in the grip of a huge snow dump and my boss, Mike Reason, declared it a day off, I pulled out my old cross-country skis and skied from Tunbridge Wells to Seven Oaks, where I caught a train to Charing Cross, drawing a few stares from local commuters. I then went by tube to the office and when I walked in the only one there was Mike. He looked at me and said, 'You've got to be kidding', and I said, 'Nope, you just can't keep me away.'

At 5 o'clock one evening I received a phone call at home to say there had been a dreadful accident on the *East Enders* set at Elstree Studios: in a stunt with a fast car the vehicle had slid out of control and pinned a cameraman to the wall by his knees. I separated everyone into different rooms and interviewed them individually about what had happened. The cameraman had to undergo surgery for crushed kneecaps and I interviewed him in hospital. The producer said he didn't see anything, which meant 'You can't indict me'. I was only 32 years old but I had to find out the truth of what happened.

The stunt coordinator had replaced a sick stuntman with a guy who had no experience. The vehicle, borrowed from the *Top Gear* set, had only a few kilometres on the clock. They'd put diesel on the road to generate smoke and make the tyres spin and the car's profile was really low to the ground. To make matters worse, camera cables strewn across the road were dragged into the vehicle's wheels as it made a fast turn. The Health and Safety Executive was going to prosecute the BBC, the stuntman and the executive producer for a breach of the Health and Safety at Work Act 1974, under both corporate and individual acts or omissions, which is a criminal safety charge, but the case never made it to trial and a severe dressing down by a senior HSE inspector was accepted by the BBC in place of a prosecution. In this case, the coordinator had allowed the bad stunt to go ahead but as time went on these types of accidents became less and less common.

A terrible accident which occurred before my time at the BBC was another key factor that changed safety and security in the industry. On *The Late, Late Breakfast Show*, Noel Edmonds would welcome everyone live on air at 7 p.m., then spin a huge wheel to land on an activity for a viewer to perform. On 13 November 1986, volunteer Michael Lush was rehearsing for a stunt called 'Hang 'em High', which involved bungy jumping from an exploding box suspended from a 120-foot crane. He jumped to his death.

When I was asked to take another look at this tragic incident I was shocked to discover that there had been no stunt coordinator or safety officer present on the day of the jump; no one had been supervising the event from up in the bucket of the crane. Michael was found dead with the bungy rope and twist lock safety carabiner lying beside him. He'd either forgotten to clip the carabiner into an anchor point, because he was caught up in the moment, or quite possibly the carabiner had opened up due to the bungy running across the gate.

Having taken a few days to digest the content of the report, I was aghast at all the things that had gone wrong and provided an additional report, based on my military experience, which was subsequently used to develop the first TV production safety course. BBC management created a Safety Services Department and I was recruited to oversee all high-risk activities. I made it my mission that nothing would slip past me. I'd say to the producers and directors, 'Tell me what you want to do.' They'd describe all these amazing things they were planning. I'd say, 'I'm here to advise you but you have to take responsibility for your actions.' It changed a lot in the industry and led to huge investigations into other incidents.

My BBC career was really taking off. Tracie, however, felt the opposite. I was hardly home and she was left to look after Brianna. I felt really torn. On the one hand, I'd persuaded Tracie to move to London for an exciting new life away from the monotonous routine of Plymouth; on the other hand, I just couldn't be there to support her. To make matters worse, she knew no one in London and even fewer in Tunbridge Wells, where she'd insisted we move so she could be near her best friend Sue, who was in fact spending more time with her new boyfriend. In short, my life was exciting and Tracie's was quite pedestrian.

***

The next project I embarked on was one of the most pivotal and influential pieces of safety work in the media industry and served as the bedrock for the high-risk safety and security support company, ZeroRisk, that I would found in 2002. This kind of training was desperately needed. Too many young actors, production crew and members of the public were being badly injured or killed as a result of stunts and events going wrong. To champion this cause, we had three heavy hitters in the safety world, Gavin Birkett, Harry Muir and Bill Carver, a no-nonsense film director, raised in the Bronx and perfectly positioned to interpret how productions cut corners on film sets.

Gavin and Bill came up with the idea of a four-part safety film, to be used by the BBC, but also rolled out to the entire media and film industry. It would follow a young production runner called Kate and the difficulties she faced fitting into the production groove with all its prejudices and egos. Philip Bretherton, from the BBC sit com, *As Time Goes By*, played the lead role of Anthony, a vicious, aggressive and dangerous director, and Julie T. Wallace, from the TV drama *Life and Times of a She-Devil*, played an aspiring actress who would do anything for Anthony if it meant fame and glory. The stunts got bigger and more dangerous, resulting in an accident on set and a court case for potential corporate manslaughter.

The film was an instant hit with BBC executives but went way over budget to the tune of £1,000,000. Back in the 1990s that was a lot of money. Mike Reason, head of the BBC Safety Division, took this on the chin but I'll never forget his face when we invited him onto the film set. It was winter and we were set up in a dark, wet alleyway next to a disused warehouse. When the first 'Action' cue was given, a large gas tanker spewed out its lit content and you could feel the fireball licking all around you. Then came a stunt bike, popping a wheelie all the way through the flames and halting right next to Mike, who stood there speechless, glasses fogged up and ash and rain falling all over his green tweed jacket. 'Er, thanks for having me, everybody, and good luck with the project,' he said. I knew there and then that he'd never be seen on set again.

With the film finished, it was time to develop the training material and I was charged with developing four training modules based on different scenarios: 'The Floor Manager's Tale' – her vulnerabilities and how the crew let her down; 'The Production Manager's Tale' – weak or strong, responsible or not for safety; 'The Director's Tale'

– character analysis and this role's responsibility; and 'The Executive Producer's Tale' – as above but this time the executive producer, the floor manager and the production manager were in court.

Occupational law featured heavily in the safety qualification I was finishing and I relished applying what I'd learnt to this course. I made part four as close as possible to a real courtroom and began to explore the legal concept of acts and omissions and the crazy part of English law that reverses the burden of proof: you're guilty until proven innocent. My training syllabus revolved around past accidents in the TV and film industry, analysing what went wrong and explaining the risk assessment process that would help to prevent such things happening again.

The course was a massive hit and for the first time in the industry, safety training became engaging, exciting and relevant. To me it was a *Dead Poets Society* moment. Our safety risk analysis team noticed rates of accidents and incidents tumble in the BBC drama and light entertainment division, and the health and safety inspectors reduced the amount of unannounced site visits.

My two-year contract was coming to an end but, thanks to Mike, I was made permanent and to my delight, in August 1993, came the move into news. My joy was tinged with sadness, however, as by then Tracie and I had split, and she had moved back to Plymouth with Brianna. She wanted to be close to her mother and family and I couldn't give up the BBC life. I went down to Plymouth every other weekend and even applied for a job at South West Water, but the manager took one look at my CV and said, 'For God's sake, man, you're working for the BBC. Anyone would snap your arm off for that position.' I agreed with him but explained that I was trying to save my marriage and needed to find work closer to Plymouth and my family. He said to me, 'Look Tony, follow your dream.' I knew he was right. I was starting to form my own identity for the first time since leaving the military. I returned to Plymouth and told Tracie that although I would do everything I could to make the marriage work, I wasn't going to look for a job in Exeter or Plymouth.

Things didn't get any easier. After six months of commuting, I asked Tracie to move back up to London and she refused. That really was the final blow for our relationship, which would end in divorce. I still saw Brianna every few weeks and made Bristol the halfway point for pick-ups and drop-offs. My young daughter loved coming up to London and always wanted to spend more time with me.

During 1993 and 1994 I threw my heart and soul into work. I went out on the road a lot and really got to understand what each person did on location. With this knowledge I started formulating safety policy, guidelines and procedures for high-risk activities. One, which covered working in cold weather, drew a few laughs when I explained that if you detected frostnip while on location, you should place your hands in the armpits or crotch of one of your colleagues. This, and other guidelines, were givens in the commando world but initially met with suspicion in the TV and film industry. It also became apparent to the management I was more useful working out of Television Centre (TVC), where all news operations were based. News editor Richard Sambrook and Vin Ray, head of international news, lobbied my boss Peter Hunter, head of news safety, to let me have a desk in the much-respected news management suites of Room 6500 in Wood Lane. My wish was granted and I was given a desk in a pod of four. Directly in front of me was Nicholas Witchell, the BBC's royal correspondent.

Despite my career going from strength to strength, however, I felt lost and as if my daughter was gone. In my mid-thirties, I was living in London with no real close friends. I'd settled into a rental place with three doctors, all of whom drank like fish and partied hard. Single once again, I could have regressed to the social life of my mid-twenties but instead I threw myself into exercise, particularly running and swimming. I also volunteered for anything at work.

CHAPTER 9
HOSTILE ENVIRONMENTS

IN JUNE 1995, I moved to BBC White City, a new building right in the middle of a socially deprived and highly dangerous area on South Africa Road: the day the BBC occupied the new building, shots were fired from the flats and glass was smashed. My new office, on the first floor, was directly opposite the BBC Current Affairs division, which meant I could stroll down the road to the newsroom and drop in on any documentary planning meetings.

By this time, I had met my new partner, Jill. This had happened by chance at London Weekend Television, where she worked as an HR manager. I was taken by her warm and friendly manner but as my interaction was with the safety department, we barely made contact. It was at another LWT meeting that I discovered Jill was an excellent middle-distance runner and we decided to meet at night and jog around Stanmore, where I was living. We soon bonded and Jill introduced me to her family. She was living in Belsize Park, much closer to my office in White City, and after dating for 18 months we decided to move in together and rented a house on the edge of Regent's Park, close to our favourite pub, The World's End, and the iconic music venue, Electric Ballroom. We lived there happily for a few years, before buying a flat close to Hampstead Heath. That was where we were living when our daughter Katie was born in 1996. When we thought Jill was in labour, we rushed into the nearby Royal Free Hospital, only to be told that it wasn't time and we should walk around a bit. I immediately hit on the great idea of wandering through the house of one of my favourite poets, John Keats, which stands on Hampstead Heath. And it was while we were looking at a glass cabinet housing the manuscript of 'Ode to a Nightingale' that Jill's waters broke and we made the short walk back to the Royal Free.

The Bosnian War was still raging. The Croats were claiming their land back and the Bosnian Serbs, headed up by Radovan Karadžić and Ratko Mladić (both responsible for the torture and deaths of may Croats), were not giving up easily. Years later Karadžić would be indicted at The Hague for war crimes. The conflict was a turning point for British journalists; it is a little-known fact that more British journalists than peacekeepers were killed during the war.

On 31 July a group of journalists based in Zagreb received a tip-off that a peace agreement was going to be signed in the field. BBC cameraman Adam Kelleher went along with well-known foreign correspondent Jonathan Birchall, John Schofield, a 29-year-old BBC radio journalist who was working for *The World Tonight*, and Omar Asawi, a BBC World Service journalist. Having arrived in Croatia, they met with a former journalist turned logistician who arranged for them to hire an old Northern Irish vehicle, a desperate but poor choice. From my time in Belfast, I knew only too well the dangers of travelling in such vehicles. They were made of steel, which ensured that they were both extremely heavy and freezing cold during winter. It was easy to attach booby traps underneath them and they were also prone to landmine blasts that sent fragments inside the vehicle. This one had no press insignia anywhere and, significantly, carried yellow Serbian plates instead of white Croatian ones. It also looked aggressively military.

When they reached their intended destination, the town of Candzije, they sensed things weren't right. There were cows in the fields with full, unmilked udders and the grass was high, indicating that no one had inhabited the place for a considerable time. They suspected Serbian forces had conducted ethnic cleansing in and around the area, which was still not under Croat control. They arrived in the memorial park known as Abez Forest, rounded a corner, stopped and, one by one, the four journalists got out of the vehicle.

Adam put on his body armour and hoisted his heavy camera onto his shoulder to film a set of Serb-owned houses on fire in the valley below. John Schofield also donned his body armour and both he and Jonathan Birchall moved away from the vehicle and walked to the top of the track to get clean sound for a radio report. Omar Asawi climbed onto the top of the vehicle to take photos of the burning houses. Just then there was an almighty bang and automatic fire rained down on them, killing John Schofield. He was a brilliant journalist; this was a tragic loss to his family and to the BBC.

The original investigation was carried out by senior BBC news executive Ray Gowridge, who took statements from everyone involved and produced a report that went to the BBC News board. Their findings were handed to news head Chris Kramer, a tremendous advocate of journalist safety and a survivor of the 1980 Iranian embassy siege. He called me into his office. Also there was global news head Richard Sambrook, a brilliant journalist, and now Professor of Journalism and Director of the Centre for Journalism at Cardiff University.

Chris said, 'We've lost too many journalists. What do you think needs to be done?' I replied that we were sending news crews off to war zones with only battlefield first aid training under their belt. As John's death made all too clear, we weren't teaching them to recognise hazards and risks. 'In the military you would usually be given a great deal of training to enter a war zone, so why is it different for journalists?' I suggested we should explore the possibility of running a hostile environments course that would teach journalists proactive risk analysis, how to spot a landmine or a booby trap and how to react under hostile fire. Both agreed and Richard gave me a cheque. The training needed to be quite extensive to cover a whole range of subjects such as improvised explosive devices (IEDs), riots, vehicle checkpoints and other important subjects, and the course could only last two days. But it was a start. I'd already identified the need for better armoured vehicles, body armour, clothing and medical trauma kits: what they had in the store was obsolete. I also concentrated on developing deployment strategies and relevant guidance and operational procedural documents.

There would be a follow-up to John Schofield's story. In August 2002, in the office of BBC Radio head Steve Mitchell, I met John Schofield's wife, Susannah, and her six-year-old daughter, Charlotte, who was the spitting image of John. Susannah had been pregnant when John was killed and her daughter had started asking questions to which her mother really couldn't reply. She also wanted to know whether there were extenuating circumstances that might potentially point to a war crime. Susannah was involved in setting up the John Schofield Trust but she needed answers to move on with her life. This was when I discovered that the previous report about John's death didn't go into enough detail. No one really knew what happened and Steve believed it would be useful for all concerned to reopen the investigation. John's body had been left in the field for two days as the war raged around him and the details of his death contained in the report were very sketchy.

As part of my team, I called Jane Kokan, an award-winning camerawoman, director and journalist who travelled around war zones. She was part Croatian and had family there. I also had Barry 'X', an extremely meticulous forensic investigator, and photographer Saša Schmidtbauer, who was Croatian and knew everyone we needed to know. We wanted to find out John's exact movements and who was responsible for the ethnic cleansing of the area he headed to that day. I was really struggling with finding this location as all I had to go on were old photographs. So I came up with the idea of calling Adam Kelleher and inviting him over to Croatia to pinpoint where it had happened and assist me with the investigation.

Adam agreed but it wasn't easy for him. He'd suffered flashbacks for many years and now his memory took him straight back to the day. After visiting the site we returned to Zagreb and headed to a bar. Adam ordered four scotches in quick succession, announcing the first was 'for John'. White-faced and visibly shaken, he began to cry uncontrollably. He'd spent years waking up in a cold sweat, reliving the details, and had left journalism to save his marriage. Two months later, I assisted a freelance news agency to produce a compelling report on the risks of PTSD, focusing on the importance of debriefing after an accident, and of returning to the scene of a traumatic event to talk through the process and grieve.

With Adam's first-hand account, I could see how the situation might have developed. The Croats could have easily encroached on Adam and John's armoured vehicle but instead chose to halt the recce party and report back to an assault squad that a white armoured vehicle was heading towards their area. The attackers could see movement in the vehicle, and later on mentioned that a similar-looking Serbian vehicle had attacked their position the day before. But I needed concrete proof. I didn't have sign-off from the

Croatian military that could confirm who the attacking group was.

After deciding to stay on for a couple of extra months, I pursued a forensic specialised pathologist named Josip Čadež at Zagreb Hospital. Čadež had photographs of John and admitted he had been drinking as the war depressed him, which accounted for what was considered a substandard report on the state of John's body. But the report written by a pathologist in the UK when John's body arrived back in London had missed vital ballistic injuries on the body. He had not picked up that John had been hit and killed by a grenade, not by a single bullet. It was an explosive charge that blew John's chest apart.

Tests that I commissioned from Dave Leeming of the Cranfield Ordnance Test and Evaluation Centre (COTEC) in Wiltshire concluded the body armour was not fitted with a protective collar, which may have deflected the bullet that entered John's neck. The armour worn was also too short to protect the kidneys and abdomen. John had been hit by an explosive charge on the upper part of his chest in an area that was unprotected due to his armour being left open, vaporising the charge inside his body. I showed the test results to Čadež and suggested the grenade used was supposed to hit the vehicle but overshot and hit John instead. Čadež kept repeating a word that Jane explained meant a Croatian-made grenade which could be fired from the end of a rifle, and was made of copper so it could push through the armour on the vehicle.

John's death was ruled 'death by mistaken identity', the investigation was over and together with Susannah we headed to the spot where John was killed for a ceremony and the laying of a plaque. I never met John, but his death was not in vain, since it highlighted the need to review journalist safety and inspired me to dig deep on how we could provide better protection and improve the chances of survival for those who risk their lives to tell the story.

***

I made some disturbing discoveries. There was no accountability: once journalists were on assignment, the BBC didn't know where they were. I described the Balkan War as one of journalistic opportunity and convenience: any freelance reporter could pay £100 for a return flight to Macedonia, two and a half hours each way, walk across the border and be in the heat of the fighting on an ever-moving front line. I learnt that journalists begged, stole and borrowed flak jackets and helmets, some of which had already been damaged by gunshots or knife attacks or simply didn't fit properly. The body armour was too heavy. It was made of steel or ceramic, which meant that when it was fired at, the fragments would go into the neck or the face. Their first aid kits consisted of little more than a couple of Band-aids and aspirin and were often left inside their vehicles.

I also found out that staffers working for news agencies were insured when reporting from war zones but freelancers weren't. In the many conflicts that erupted during the collapse of Yugoslavia, more than 150 reporters, photographers, television camera operators, producers, fixers and other media workers were killed. It was so much worse for freelance journalists than staffers. Quite often they weren't contracted to any news network but would put their necks on the line to get that one photo, video or text – the money shot – that would shock the world and catapult their career to the next level. They were supposed to love their work and give their masters more of the bang bang, but were paid only for what they produced. Risk advisers and insurance assessors referred to it as keeping clear blue water between the network and the freelancer.

I quickly rectified this by recruiting BBC's Vin Ray and chief BBC war correspondent Kate Adie to work with me and aggressively lobby insurance companies to offer insurance to freelancers who have successfully completed hostile environment training and have experience working with news agencies. I'm pleased to say that this system is still very much in place today.

The first two-day hostile environments course, in December 1995, was held in a back room of a Sussex hotel, filled with journalists who could cover wars in their sleep and were a bit dubious when they turned up, thinking this was another insurance arse-covering exercise run by management. I quickly realised how few skills these journalists had in hostile environments. Most were masking different PTSD symptoms; one journalist wore a parka with a circle on the back. It was a proactive and lively course with many elements, such as simulated attacks, run outside the classroom. After a while, the hotel had so many noise complaints from other rooms also running courses and conferences that we had to find our own venue. Journalists from ITN, Reuters and Sky News all clamoured to do the course.

Over the first few months it was clear to me that I was going to have to draw on more expertise and then I had a lightbulb moment: I'd get in touch with my old team at the M&AW Cadre. Two former colleagues and I developed the first ever comprehensive hostile environments course for journalists. Six months after kick-starting the first course, I had a tricky time convincing management that we needed to put the BBC journalists through bigger and riskier scenarios, but somehow I always managed to secure their backing. What started off as a two-day course in a hotel quickly expanded to a four-day residential course, covering everything from dealing with a checkpoint through to how to conduct yourself if you were kidnapped or detained. I headed the training, as a BBC staffer, and delivered the course with Centurion Risk Assessment Services, whom I'd commissioned to run all BBC hostile environments courses. All training subjects were conducted via first a lesson and then a full-blown simulation with blank firing and pyrotechnics used to mimic an explosive attack. Delegates were well and truly submerged in all the scenarios: as we said to them, it was better to learn there than in Bosnia or Chechnya.

As courses came and went, all eight members of the instruction team gathered feedback from journalists on how the training had helped them. It was the experience shared by BBC World Service producer Shamsa Abdullahi Ahmed, better known as Shamsa Pay-Book, that really fuelled momentum. Had it not been for the training she received, on one of our first four-day courses, she would have been executed in Somalia, her homeland. She had flown to Mogadishu, still in the grip of civil war, to collect programme material, and she and a group of friends and relatives were held up by seven armed men, who took her to a riverbank close by. They asked, 'Which one of you is the journalist bitch?' Three of them took her aside and pressed their guns into her shoulders while another held a bayonet to her stomach.

As she told a reporter afterwards, Shamsa remembered the lessons we'd taught her. 'I began going over the advice we'd been given: don't panic, control your breathing, make eye contact, never be negative, think positive thoughts and don't ask questions. I stared so hard into the eyes of the man with the bayonet that I didn't even blink, and I kept saying to myself that everything would be all right, and that I would be with my children again.' More gunmen arrived: 'I tried to stay cool and to keep my breathing steady, but it was difficult.' Told to check the contents of the carrier bag they had taken from her, she pretended to do so and said everything was fine. Finally she was released, as long as she neither identified her captors or mentioned the incident in a broadcast. As Shamsa told us, the course saved her life.

***

The course consisted of 10 lessons, which ran as follows: deployment planning and preparation, incident management (back to base communication), weapons (live firing on a weapons range where attendees would stand still and instructors would fire over their heads), wound ballistics (treatment of gunshot wounds), IEDs from grenade to artillery fire, how to avoid kidnap and ransom and what to do if it happened (this part of the course was like a stripped down version of our military training), demonstrations and riots, reporting from natural disasters (which included tropical diseases and treatments), negotiating vehicle checkpoints (urban and rural) and PTSD and the importance of one-on-one and group debriefing.

The two days truly kicked off with a bang as transport was organised to pick everyone up from the airport and nearest train stations; there was a set rendezvous for those who drove. The trap was now set: the attendees were all in one area and we only had to wait and observe from a hedge some 100 metres away. Suddenly the air would be filled with rapid and sustained gunfire, the instructors and actors tearing through blank ammunition to deliver a shocking attack on the senses. This carefully choreographed greeting made it more than clear that they were now entering a world of constant danger and surprises. I remember the complete silence long after the last blank round was fired. If you got close enough to the delegates lying face down on the gravel track, though, you could hear them panting for breath, and see their jaws and fingers twitching feverishly in nervous spasm. The tension was palpable. Even as we escorted all the delegates to the main training building, no one uttered a word, though heads would dart from side to side, nervously waiting for what might happen next.

The trick with any hostile environments course is to keep the element of surprise fresh. Some training organisations always delivered the same formulaic outline. When, at the BBC, I contracted out all the training to private security companies whose instructors were former military, I noticed that they initially lacked any understanding of what a journalist was searching for in a story – that rush of adrenaline. These were war junkies who lived on the edge. Some security companies, too, struggled to contain the excitement and enthusiasm of their instructors, so that the scenarios became more complex and highly dangerous.

I remember with dread one moment where I thought all my hard work in setting up hostile environments training had actually gone up in flames. It was 6 p.m. on a dark and cold winter's night. The BBC doctor, whom I knew really well and was on the course, called me to say that there had been a very serious incident and I needed to come down. When I arrived, I discovered that during the set-up for one of the ambushes a senior instructor was carrying, in his right hand, a handful of military-style thunderflashes which he was about to place in the ground at strategic intervals. Without warning or explanation, they all detonated, leaving the instructor's hand hanging on by a few tendons and blowing a gaping hole in his thigh, exposing his femoral artery. The quick-thinking doctor had managed to deliver advanced first aid and had the instructor taken by air to a local hospital.

This situation highlighted many things for me, among them the fact that ex-military people might know about explosives, but they had no experience in pyrotechnics and theatrical simulation. I deduced that the pyrotechnics could have been triggered by static from the air, static from the rubbing of Gore-Tex waterproof clothing or the proximity of a mobile phone or, more likely, the VHF radio the instructor had on his belt. One other glaring concern was the fact that all pyrotechnics had two long wires protruding from the top which, when connected to a battery and a switch, would detonate the device. These wires had to be crossed and crimped; if they were left open any electrical impulse would cause detonation. Cold sweat ran down my neck. Without the swift intervention of the BBC doctor there could have been a death that day and the end of hostile environments training as we knew it.

CHAPTER 10
MR D AND D

ONE DAY IN the early part of 1995, I was summoned to the large teak-lined executive office suite of Eric 'the bad cop' Bowman, Deputy Director of News and Current Affairs. Eric fixed me with a steely-eyed gaze and said, 'Can you keep a secret?' Wondering where he was going with this, and whether I was in for some sort of initiation ceremony, I replied, 'Yes, of course.' He then said, 'I think you can. I've read your file and you navy commando blokes are something else but you'll never be better than us paras.' This was a reference to his days in the Parachute Regiment. 'Cancel everything this evening. You're going to be busy for the next few weeks and months. Report to Steve Hewlett's office over in *Panorama*.' I knew this must be something big. Steve Hewlett, affectionately known to his team as 'Cracker' because he looked like actor Robbie Coltrane, was involved only when for something extremely high profile.

At 7 p.m. I wandered over to Steve's office to be greeted by Eric, Steve and journalist Martin Bashir. They'd finished their pre-editorial meeting and signalled for me to take a seat.

Eric said, 'There are only four of us who know about this and you're now the fifth. So the way I see it, if this story gets out in the next few weeks I am going to come after your balls, navy commando boy. Do I make myself clear?'

'Crystal, para boy,' I replied.

Eric cracked a slight smile and then dropped the bombshell. 'Smart Martin here has landed the scoop of the century – a deal to interview Her Royal Highness, Princess Diana.' I sat there in stunned silence: the royals never gave interviews on this scale and a scallywag from Bootle was about to be part of an event that would go down in history. Eric explained that, to ensure the full secrecy of the interview, the BBC board of governors were not told because the chair, Marmaduke Hussey, was married to Lady Susan Hussey, a woman of the bedchamber and confidante of Queen Elizabeth. No other BBC royal journalists were informed.

As everyone now knows, there was a lot more to the story. Bashir turned out to be not very smart at all. A 2021 inquiry led by Lord Dyson concluded that he had used 'deceitful methods' and breached the rules of BBC editorial conduct to get the interview. These included using fake bank statements that appeared to reveal payments to a former security guard for Earl Spencer, Diana's brother, to induce Spencer to arrange a meeting with the princess. There had been BBC investigations in the 1990s but they were flawed and exonerated Bashir. In his report Dyson described Bashir as 'unreliable', 'devious' and 'dishonest'. At the time, though, it seemed like the most extraordinary coup and the biggest security challenge I had ever faced.

I told everyone I was up for it and would pull together a first-class security team who would give their life in support of me and the BBC. Two days later, another secret meeting kicked off with a bang as Steve explained what Diana was prepared to say on camera. We knew we had a broadcast transmission date of 20 November and Steve said that *Panorama* was moving the normal slot to a later time of 9 p.m. so we could maximise the audience. Then Eric announced, 'Tony, over to you, not just for security but the top-end stuff.' This was it, my chance to shine. I paused, then looked around once more before letting them in on the 10-point plan I'd gone over in my head a million times. It included such matters as my team and I having a BBC ID card that was off the grid and colour coded so that we would not be challenged anywhere in any BBC building, and media silence at all times.

The weirdest part about the whole thing was going about my daily life, reporting to my boss, Peter Hunter, and chatting with Jill, knowing full well I was part of a story that was about to turn a huge and unwelcome spotlight on the entire royal family. However tempting it was to say something, particularly down the pub when my mates were dissecting every piece of the Di and Charles relationship, I kept completely quiet.

My first task was to assess Kensington Palace and its surroundings as a potential interview location. Dressed as a tourist, I wandered around the perimeter, looking for main vantage points potentially used by paparazzi. I checked every approach road and areas covered by CCTV. I monitored the traffic: all approach areas most times of the day were heavily congested and the best way around would be by motorbike or scooter. My next and most important task was choosing my security team. I met with a friend, a former military colleague who had left the Marines, and gave him the basic outline. He immediately put eight highly trained and skilled surveillance and former sniper teams on task and we started rolling out the plan from there.

In the run-up to 5 November, when the interview would take place, we left no stone unturned and put in 24/7 surveillance at Martin Bashir's house, the BBC Television Centre, Kensington Palace and a building we'd lined up for the programme editing.

The days and nights were gruelling as we arranged surveillance and regularly checked for paparazzi. With just hours to go to the interview, I had a tip-off from a contact in Fleet Street telling me, without being aware of what we were up to, that any royal story would attract a huge fee for the smallest of titbits. It was intimated that print media, in particular, would pay up to £1,000,000 for the slightest sound bite of a really big breaking news story. This put me on high alert and the risk clock started ticking.

There was immense relief when Martin finished the interview. We had advised that only one trusted BBC cameraman, Tony Poole, be used and he could shoot the interview on two cameras, which would give the editor more material to work with. This worked really well and reduced any potential for suspicion. The BBC camera equipment was also introduced into Kensington Palace as state-of-the-art hi-fi equipment to avoid any suspicion.

As Martin pulled out of Kensington Palace, my security team did the follow-up and from then on we worked tirelessly to maintain 100 per cent security. I visited the edit suite every day and can still hear Diana's voice coming out of the old Beta recorders. Locked in my memory is the sadness of the princess, who appeared shaken but resolute, relieved that everything was out in the open. The decision was made to move the final edit to TVC in Shepherd's Bush. There was one final thing left to do, which caused contention at the BBC, but we'd come this far and couldn't fail at the final hurdle. I pushed to have the usual contract guard force removed from TVC and used my handpicked and trusted team to provide all the security for the inner part of the building and the most vulnerable edit suites. In the final days before the broadcast, which had by now been trailered, we had dummy taxis and Martin Bashir and Diana lookalikes whizzing around London. By 20 November we were exhausted but buzzing. The programme shocked the nation and the world.

***

Between 1995 and 1997 I spent a lot of time in Northern Ireland working with BBC's Northern Ireland dream team, reporter Denis Murray and cameraman Mark McCauley. Both were seasoned journalists with a great eye for detail and high-level contacts, politically and with the IRA, the Ulster Volunteer Force and the Ulster Defence Association. I'd of course worked on the streets in Northern Ireland in my military days. There's a scene from that time that still haunts me and one I talk about on hostile environments training programmes. As I rounded a corner for protection in Belfast's Shankhill Road, I witnessed a very young female radio reporter retreating from a volley of petrol bombs and finding shelter in the doorway of a house. She appeared to be fumbling with her radio equipment and didn't notice the first petrol bomb crashing down at her feet. This time there was no flame, just shattered glass and the smell of petrol. Before I could take two steps to alert her of the danger, another two petrol bombs shattered on the pavement and a 6-metre flame lit up the street and the poor journalist. Her colleagues stood there with their mouths wide open, not knowing what to do, as she was burnt alive. It was two of our crew who threw her to the ground and extinguished the flame.

What stood out to me that day was how poorly prepared and naive some of the journalists were. They didn't know you should never stand in a doorway with your back to the wall when petrol bombs are being thrown as the sheer heat feeding on the trapped air in the entrance intensifies and engulfs anything and anyone in its wake. The worst thing you can do is leave someone standing if they're on fire because the flames burn the inside of the mouth and the trachea, causing swelling and asphyxia.

Fast forward 10 years and I was with the journalists, with no weapon, no body armour and no one to watch my back. I felt deeply exposed and vulnerable and survived purely on instinct and adrenaline. I learnt another important journalist truth during this time: while everyone else was running away from violent protesters and trouble, news crews often ran towards the danger. Thankfully that attitude would be replaced by the approach of the highly regarded Chris Kramer: 'No story is worth a life.'

In 1995, with 12 July looming, I went from Belfast to Drumcree with the BBC crew to work out the best and safest positions to report news from. The Twelfth, as it's often known, is the day when Ulster Protestants march to mark Protestant William of Orange's victory over deposed Catholic king James II of England, and VII of Scotland, in the Battle of the Boyne back in 1690. The day is a touchpaper for violence between Protestants and Catholics. Not only did I have to look after the BBC Northern Ireland crew but it looked like the news-gathering bosses wanted to put more crew on the ground. This raised concerns for me as it increased the risk of serious injury during the march.

Tensions were really high when we carried out a walk-through on the evening of the 11th. As we moved around the roads, we witnessed car after car set on fire, obviously sacrificed to create a roadblock. We were conscious of being watched and followed and were mindful that anything we said could potentially inflame the crowds. One wrong turn of a phrase and we'd be attacked and seriously injured. We tried to get some rest that night but the noise of objects being moved around, fires being lit and shouts and screams from youths close to our vehicles proved too much. The team and I managed three hours of sleep at best.

The following morning brought more noise, more violent activities and a massive intervention from the police. The tension continued to mount, and we found ourselves dodging household furniture, nappies and bricks being thrown and catapults fired in our general direction. Based on my knowledge of working in riots, I provided teams with the best advice possible but our biggest problem was knowing where everyone was and getting the camera tapes (these were pre-digital times) back to a satellite truck so we could feed the package directly into the BBC newsroom.

The bombings, shootings and rioting we experienced were off the scale but somehow we all managed to survive. Apart from a few minor injuries and exhaustion, it was considered a job well done. After a debrief with the team in Belfast, I travelled back to London and got to work on changing 'Safety in Demonstrations' forever. My first port of call was Larry, now in security, who happened to be a former public order instructor in the Metropolitan Police. He invited me to a meeting at their Public Order Training HQ in Hounslow, built out of film stage flats but for all intents and purposes an operational village. I was completely in awe of this set-up, which had been sanctioned by Margaret Thatcher as a result of the 1984 miners' strike and the poll tax riots in 1990. The training we eventually agreed on was really well received and became mandatory in the BBC. We taught half a day of theory before journalists walked onto the training ground at night, encountering actors playing rioters. Horses charged back and forth, water cannon were deployed and wooden blocks and petrol bombs were thrown.

One evening I took the BBC bosses down to the training ground, where Larry had organised for all of us to stand at the top of one building for a bird's-eye view of the village. No sooner had we taken up our positions than we heard a fog horn, which was the signal for the training to begin. Like gladiators, the police arrived with their short shields, followed by angry protesters and a large number of armoured personnel carriers. Then in the distance we spotted a band of stick figures dressed in blue tabards with the word

'PRESS' emblazoned on their uniforms. As soon as they appeared, all hell broke loose. Missiles were flying everywhere, protesters were grabbing our crew and spinning them around like rag dolls, swearing at them.

***

After refining and introducing the training I went to work on the complete lack of coordination between the news desk in HQ and crews on the ground in a demonstration. In addition, multiple news crews were turning up to film the same incident. My resolution in this area proved invaluable during May Day protests in London in 2001 when the new protocol stopped all the BBC news crews being hemmed in behind a police containment line.

News crews were also turning up for demonstrations with little or no protective gear. I wanted them covered head to toe but didn't want them to feel restricted in any way. They had to be free to move quickly. I researched a lot of personal protective equipment (PPE) and came up with kit that's now considered mandatory across all news agencies when covering a demonstration. We moved to jet ski-style goggles, which gave the team protection against missiles being thrown and from liquid and mist substances, including tear gas. We discovered they gave you 180-degree vision and with the correct lens treatment wouldn't fog up when you were running for safety or covering a story during a demo. They would prove a success during major demonstrations in Athens at the 2004 Olympic Games, when tear gas was liberally used to disperse anti-capitalist protests.

We also developed a tough plastic insert to go into any baseball cap to prevent injuries caused by flying glass and bricks. As BBC's Jeremy Bowen found out, it gave him protection from kids firing heated marbles out of catapults while he was working in Gaza. During the 2007 APEC riots in Sydney, this innovation stopped a number of darts thrown by protesters from entering the skull of a cameraman during an interview with a police commander. The police commander wasn't that lucky.

The next breakthrough was the respirator. I'd often cringe seeing people wearing heavy rubber military-style gas masks with limited vision. The solution was a lightweight mask that just covered your mouth and nose and could be used in a number of circumstances in conjunction with the goggles. I turned to the industrial-style Sundström mask, which was not only light but, with its interchangeable filters, offered great protection against a range of gases, vapours, dusts and mists. News crews have used it successfully when reporting on asbestos- and anthrax-related stories.

Too many journalists were getting burnt and catching on fire. The BBC's props department came up with an anti-flammable solution called Flame Check, which could be used on TV sets to stop them catching fire. From that moment on, news crews would have one designated set of clothes, used only when reporting demonstrations, which would be soaked in Flame Check, offering brilliant protection against flame. When BBC reporter Clarence Mitchell was doing a piece to camera outside the Turkish embassy in London, a woman protesting behind him set herself on fire. He survived the close encounter.

Camera crew also now wear BMX-style elbow pads because protesters would prey on the fact that they couldn't see anything while filming and so would often attack them from behind or to the side. They have, too, stab vests, largely under their clothing when covering extremely high-risk situations where there are edged weapons, including screwdrivers and knives.

I fought long and hard, too, for security back watchers (SBW).

Some of the BBC old guard thought we were going over the top, but the SBW is now the most important safety asset when planning to film or record from any demonstration. The SBW is not only the eyes and ears of the crew but provides a high standard of medical cover and generally carries all first aid kits, water and food.

***

My mighty workload with the BBC, where I was tagged Mr D and D (Death and Destruction), was placing an enormous strain on my relationship with Jill. It was no great secret that we were both highly ambitious: Jill had landed a top job as senior HR manager for the BBC World Service. We were also raising Katie, and it wasn't easy. Jill was unimpressed by my long working hours and told me I was married to my work, not my family. I thought I was indispensable and that nothing at work could ever be achieved without me. Sucked into the BBC News machine, I created a job that no one else could do: I made myself indispensable. I would sit there and stare at my phone or wait for my pager to go off as this meant another job, another tough but interesting and secret assignment that would take me away from my family time and time again. Even at social functions, I would spend most of my time outside, trying to run through the security risks of a story on Al-Qaeda or the latest on a government leak of highly sensitive information. It became a drug; I'd sold my soul to the BBC. Looking back, I think I was too emotionally ill equipped to deal with the pressures of family life and the all-consuming role of being a BBC 'lifer'. But Jill and I were about to experience something nightmarish that would require us to draw on all our strength to stay together.

One night in December 1996, Jill mentioned that she'd love to go out for a drink with her friend Caroline and could I babysit. Around

10.30 p.m. I made sure Katie was asleep in her cot and then headed for bed. I crashed out and didn't even hear Jill coming in. In the dead of night I was awoken by a small nudge from Jill, who leant over and whispered quietly in my ear that there was a man standing at the end of our bed. I thought I was dreaming and turned over to go back to sleep, but then noticed the whites of a pair of eyes looking at me. I threw off the bedcovers and my body kicked into flight mode. The intruder, a stocky black man, sprinted down the hallway and I gave chase. He leapt through an open sash window in the bathroom; I dived after him and caught up with him as he was scaling the large wooden back fence. He didn't count on that part of the fence being rotten; it gave way under his weight, palings landing across his body. Seizing the moment, I launched myself into the air, crashing down to pin the fence, and him, to the ground. I'd completely forgotten I was naked, so I was crouching over him, legs akimbo, with my wedding tackle hanging above his face.

When I took one foot off the fence, the robber wriggled free and I felt him clutching at my balls. Then out of nowhere came a huge, right-fisted hammer blow to the side of my nose. The sensation of my nose being broken was very familiar; it had happened twice before. My head spun and everything around me was a blur. At that point I really lost the plot, picking up and hurling anything I could reach – garden furniture, plant pots and ornamental gnomes – until I got the guy back on the ground and placed him in a headlock. A shape descended on us. It was Jill, who had picked up the heaviest kitchen frying pan and was trying to whack the intruder on the head. I was managing to avoid the first hit when I saw a policeman arriving and heard the crackle of his VHF radio.

By 7 a.m., the ordeal was over and I had given a statement to the best of my ability. The police, who had congratulated me, then spotted some of my military artefacts around the walls, including my commando dagger, presented to me by the M&AW Cadre team, and started laughing. 'Fuck me, of all the houses this guy had to pick.' When the police dropped me off at the Royal Free Hospital, the casualty doctor took one look and said, 'This is a nasty fracture but I can put your nose back for you under local anaesthetic.' I agreed, but what a mistake. He grabbed my nose, without administering any anaesthetic, yanked it down and to the left so that it was lying across my cheek, then buggered off, leaving me battered, bruised and looking like something out of a Picasso painting.

The police were great and our neighbours were very kind and supportive. We tried our best to maintain a normal life and routine but Jill was traumatised; she really suffered and didn't like me leaving the house. Two days later a police squad car turned up at our home and I feared the worst. We'd heard of court cases where the robber sued the house owner for using excessive force. But we were told that our criminal was extremely violent and had been stealing to fuel his meth habit. When I received a call in January 1997 from the head of London's Metropolitan Police, congratulating me and asking me to attend Scotland Yard for a presentation of a police commendation for my role, I politely declined. They insisted, however, and eventually sent me the certificate in the post.

CHAPTER 11
MAYHEM FOR A NEW MILLENNIUM

SUNDAY, 6 FEBRUARY 2000 began as a slow news day at the BBC in London, as everyone continued to work through the tail end of a wet and miserable winter. But then at 10 a.m. I heard through my counter-terrorist contacts that an Ariana Afghan Airlines Boeing 727, Flight 805, had taken off early that morning, British time, from Afghanistan's capital, Kabul, bound for the city of Mazār-e Sharīf. But after only about quarter of an hour, contact with the plane and its pilots had been lost. It emerged later that nine armed men had taken control of the aircraft. The plane then flew to Tashkent in Uzbekistan, Aktyubinsk in Kazakhstan and then Sheremetyevo International Airport near Moscow, refuelling and releasing hostages at each stop. Twenty-three were freed. The aircraft, with some 164 people onboard, then headed for Britain. It was about 1 a.m. when Stansted staff learnt that the hijacked plane could be coming their way. It landed an hour later in an area just to the south of the airport. At 6.30 a.m. the hijackers allowed the use of a generator to run air conditioning on board and the delivery of drinks, tea bags, toilet rolls and baby food. Flights due to leave Stansted from 7 a.m. were cancelled, leaving 2000 people stranded. Hundreds of police and security personnel were placed on standby at the airport, as the negotiations with the gunmen began.

I was sent with the first wave of journalists to assess the security situation and offer the best and safest vantage point for the BBC team. When we arrived I met my long-time friend and colleague Issam Ikirmawi, a dear friend and one of the most respected BBC World Service Arabic correspondents, who was reporting for Al Jazeera. We both paused and looked at each other before I said, 'Can you believe we've got a hijacking on our hands? Who do you think is behind this?' Issam reckoned it was too early to tell but possible indicators pointed to Al-Qaeda. As soon as he said this, I thought to myself, 'We're in for the long haul', and I was right: the siege went on for five very long days.

No sooner had the aircraft been guided to the pre-positioned space next to one of the hangars than the heavens opened and the ground around us became a mass of slimy mud. I could see movement in the aircraft's cockpit but found it difficult to make out anything in the main cabin. Immediately we went into action and, as usual, the BBC Resources team, consisting of camera and sound, and engineers who drove and operated the technical live links vehicles, kicked in and set up all the technical broadcast areas, which offered us the best live reporting positions. You could see that the bright lights from our position were causing problems for the police and military trying to handle the crisis and we were moved back. We provided pictures of the aircraft and adjacent hangar and using a thermal imagery system called FLIR (Forward Looking InfraRed) we managed to capture an array of police snipers getting into position behind a nearby bush. As soon as these images were cleared by the police we were allowed to broadcast them on the evening news bulletins.

From the green grainy night imagery, we could also make out the hijackers, who were carrying pistols and ordering passengers to carry food onto the plane. Five hostages had been released not long before noon and some three hours later three more were freed. In return the authorities handed over grilled fish, roast chicken, soft drinks and bread. What the hijackers didn't know was that the counter-terrorism team had managed to secrete small hidden cameras in the food trays. This meant that the hijack leaders could be seen, standing up close to the flight deck, looking tired and extremely nervous. At this point, no one could determine what the demands or ransoms were and the hijacking continued to drift on with little negotiation and no sign of an intervention.

As the drama unfolded, I was able to draw upon one of my contacts, Rusty, who had recently left 22 SAS. Rusty was able to pass on a few hints as to how the SAS's plans were unfolding to take control of the aircraft if the police passed control to the military. Also working with me was Larry. We'd all worked together on a number of previous security incidents and I had their trust. I was then able to impart information to the BBC News team, particularly regarding how the police and medical teams could gauge stress levels on the aircraft, and how they could obtain images inside the cabin and determine who the hostage takers were. I could also advise on what external signs the aircraft displayed that would allow the security teams to determine when an assault could take place. I could make it clear, too, that, contrary to what most people might think – 'Oh, they need to bring in the SAS' – in fact it's the police who have ultimate control in such a situation. Only when they can't manage any more is it handed over to the military.

During the night on day four the plane's captain and crew managed to scramble out the cockpit window behind the backs of the hijackers and climb down from the plane on a rope ladder. On the fifth day, at 3 a.m., the steps of the plane descended and 85 people, 21 of them children, emerged, their hands in the air. The last

65 hostages were released at 6 a.m. and the hijackers surrendered to the police. No shots were fired, no storming of the aircraft was triggered and the whole sorry and terrifying episode, Britain's longest airport hijack, thankfully came to an abrupt end.

Early in 2002, the nine men, led by brothers Ali and Mohammed Safi, members of the Young Intellectuals of Afghanistan whose original intention was to flee the Taliban regime, were found guilty of hijacking and of falsely imprisoning passengers and crew and possessing grenades and firearms. Ali Safi told the court that they had come to Britain to save their lives and had taken so long to release the passengers and surrender because they were afraid. The brothers were both jailed for five years. Of the rest, six were jailed for 30 months and a seventh for 27 months.

Through our many contacts in counter-terrorism, Larry, Rusty and I were able to glean first-hand information on every step of the ordeal and carefully and securely brief the BBC correspondents. During those tiring and extremely monotonous five days, I kept everyone informed of what we knew, and this extra knowledge greatly enhanced the coverage of the story. To this day I'm eternally grateful to Larry and Rusty for their invaluable insights into a highly secretive world.

***

In late May 2000, I was in the Orkney Islands, conducting a series of deep dives with the BBC's *Blue Planet* research team on several German battleships that had been scuttled in June 1919 in the cold, deep waters of Scapa Flow. One day I was cleaning my diving equipment when Adrian Van Klaveren, head of BBC news-gathering, called the hotel. I immediately knew something was wrong as communication wasn't easy where we were – there was no mobile phone signal or phone boxes. One of the BBC's local drivers in Lebanon, Abed Takkoush, had been killed on 23 May while the team was trying to cover the tactical withdrawal of the Israel Defense Forces (IDF) from Lebanon. Nobody was really sure of the circumstances surrounding the incident but it was clear I would be jetting from Edinburgh to Beirut as quickly as possible, though I would need a quick stopover at Heathrow to pick up some spare clothes, my forensic bag, my digital camera and my binoculars. Adrian Wells, planning editor for BBC News, was to accompany me.

After many plane changes, Adrian and I arrived in Beirut around 5 p.m. At the airport, we passed through the first and second set of customs and started the lengthy process of clearing police and military checkpoints, then the final customs. The sense of mistrust and curiosity was tangible. At this point the border guards went mad, screaming for me to hit the ground, spitting and pointing to my passport, asking me why I was a Zionist pig. It all got very ugly and the hardest part was the fact that Adrian and everyone else had gone through the checkpoint and I had no one to translate for me. The guards made me face the counter and spread my legs. Using the insides of their hands like blades, they searched me thoroughly, all the while accusing me of being a spy.

After a tense 15 minutes, which seemed like a lifetime, I was pulled up from the ground and marched to one of the police cubicles. It was here that my interrogation began. I still didn't know what I'd done to cause so much offence. But as they slapped my passport on the table in front of me, something caught my eye. In the centre, in the corner where the page folded, was an Israeli stamp from a decade ago. Shit, I thought, I'd travelled to the port city of Eilat on a dive. They were trying to get me to sign some kind of document, and as soon as one of the guys disappeared, I quickly leant over to look at it. It was some kind of nonsensical false confession that made me extremely nervous.

Luckily for me, an imposing Arabic-speaking guy with huge hands knew my dear friend, Issam Ikirmawi. Somehow this man was already aware that the BBC was coming to investigate why the driver had been killed – he knew Abed Takkoush – and he was able to corroborate my story. He had me released as soon as he could and welcomed me to Lebanon and to Hezbollah, the Islamist resistance group. As he left me at the front of the airport, he said, 'If you need anything, please call me and talk to my office.' As bad and as brief as my interrogation ordeal had been, things could have been even worse: Adrian had £20,000 in his briefcase, given to him by Chris Kramer at the BBC to pay for Abed's funeral costs. Chris was a true leading light in looking after the drivers, fixers and freelancers who often put their lives on the line for us.

We visited Abed's family and attended his funeral, then got on with the investigation as we didn't have much time. With the help of Chris Cobb-Smith, a colleague of mine who was a first-class military specialist and flew into Tel Aviv, my own examination and witness statements and footage from other journalists, I was able to put together what had happened. The BBC's chief Middle East correspondent, Jeremy Bowen, cameraman Malek Kenaan and Abed Takkoush had been travelling in a car first thing in the morning. As they were heading towards the Lebanese border, Jeremy decided to stop and get out to record an interview. Abed stayed behind the wheel; Malek popped the boot, put the TV camera on his shoulder and started to walk down the hill. A tank round was fired – a heat round locked onto the heat from the vehicle's exhaust pipe – and Abed was immediately set on fire, as the flame created blew out the back end of the car. Abed, who had been on the phone to his eight-year-old son, had spent 22 years working in conflict zones.

Chris and I were able to identify the tank. An army radio operator based on the hill overlooking Abed's vehicle position across the border in Lebanon was responsible for directing the tank fire onto the target and giving the order to open fire. The Israelis denied all knowledge and said that Hezbollah fired on the vehicle by mistake, but we now had proof to the contrary.

Jeremy felt sick and very guilty. (He and his team suffered dreadful PTSD.) He told me he wanted to get a reverse camera shot and that's why he left the vehicle; Malek had by then put his tripod up ready to film some great footage. The Israelis saw them getting out of their vehicle and believed they looked like Hezbollah. They also stated that they thought they could see an anti-tank weapon, which in fact was Malek's camera. Putting a tripod on the ground looking at the Israeli position was a hostile move; even the other journalists posted high on the hill on the Israeli side commented on this. It would have definitely looked like a mortar base plate position that might be going to fire into the Israeli community. None of the BBC team checked if the countryside was live. There was no communication: the crew separated themselves from the driver, who had parked the car in an open and very exposed area. We discovered other problems. The vehicle wasn't marked as media. The men weren't wearing body armour. The medical trauma pack or first aid kit, satellite phone and body armour were buried in the boot of the vehicle when the tank round struck.

Jeremy and his wife Julia were both instrumental in getting an interview with the IDF, who confirmed they thought he and the crew were terrorists because Hezbollah were fleeing the area during an agreed Israeli tactical withdrawal. The Israelis also told me that the movement of people getting out the vehicle and seeing what looked like a small rocket launcher (in fact the camera and tripod) gave them reason to believe it was the beginning of an attack from the Lebanese side. They also said that, originally, they thought the vehicle had been hit by a Hezbollah anti-tank weapon.

The whole debacle really showed me how vital hostile environment training was. On the back of my report, BBC management hammered this point. From then on anyone deploying to a such a place had to prove they'd attended and completed a hostile environment course by showing a certificate. As Chris Kramer said, 'No show, no go.'

* * *

In mid-2000, I was back in Northern Ireland, working in Londonderry planning news coverage and safety for another round of sectarian marches, when BBC reporter Tom Mangold informed me that our close colleague, reporter and investigator John Ware, had convinced the BBC and *Panorama* bosses to investigate an extraordinary claim – that, at the time of the 15 August 1998 Omagh bombing, the British intelligence agency, Government Communications Headquarters, was monitoring conversations between the bombers as the bomb was being driven into Omagh. Shortly after, I was summoned back to London for a meeting with the newly appointed editor of *Panorama*, Peter Horrocks, and John Ware, unmistakable with his white shock of hair and baggy linen jacket.

After a sort of Mexican stand-off between the three of us, eyes flicking, checking out one another's body posture for any sign of weakness, Peter broke the ice. 'John, I've explained to Tony that whatever you say from now on will be kept in the strictest of confidence.' John relaxed his crossed arms slightly and dropped his shoulders. 'He'd better. It's taken me months to get this far.' He then quizzed me on Northern Ireland. I think he was reassured by my knowledge and investigation work and the large database of security contacts I could draw on around the globe and particularly in Ireland. Once I'd finished speaking, I noticed John's arms were no longer folded and he reached for his notepad with a sense of ease.

Whatever happened after that meeting had to be the best kept secret on the planet: Omagh was still raw and threatening to derail the 10 April 1998 Good Friday Agreement. The IRA were unforgiving and ruthless. We would need a lot of high-level security protection for John, his family and everyone else involved.

Without wasting any time, I called my old Belfast contact, Paddy, formerly with the E4A, the intelligence-gathering unit of the Royal Ulster Constabulary, and arranged to see him in Belfast the following day. We met at the Europa in Great Victoria Street, which still carries the unenviable title of Europe's most bombed hotel. I got down to business, explaining what we were trying to do and stressing that we couldn't discuss the story with anyone, including the BBC Belfast crew. The fear was someone at the office could have links to the IRA. Paddy called me the following day and confirmed he was in.

As the investigation got fully under way I would be based in my own safe house in Northern Ireland, contactable only by secure communications. This also meant that John and the team could get on with doing what they did best, telling the story. Paddy managed his team so well that, in all the days out on the road, they were compromised only a few times and managed to pull out before the heavies arrived. Paddy had all the best surveillance equipment, or rigs as it's called, and everything ran like clockwork: surveillance on houses, working areas, pubs, restaurants and even the occasional wedding. The information would flow to me via Paddy and in turn I'd feed this back to Peter Horrocks and his fellow executives.

The 45-minute programme went to air in October 2000 to rave reviews and the following year John Ware and the *Panorama* team won a Royal Television Society Award for their brave investigative journalism. But the IRA did come after John and the BBC. Intimidation of the Ware family resulted in my team conducting 24/7 surveillance for months and even fitting anti-tamper detection devices on John's and his wife's cars. The equipment was triggered a few times. What freaked us out most was learning that an oven had been delivered to John's home address without him or his wife having ordered it. We thought then that things would ramp up again and they did.

On 4 March 2001, as I was belatedly celebrating my thirty-ninth birthday, I received a pager message that a situation was unfolding right outside BBC Television Centre in Shepherd's Bush. A red taxi had been left outside the main reception at 11 p.m. on 3 March. At 12.27 a.m. on the 4th a bomb, consisting of some 5–10 kilos of high explosive, exploded in the boot. Staff had already been evacuated after police received a coded warning and there were no fatalities. The main facade of the building was buckled and bent, windows were smashed and the walls adjoining Wood Lane tube station levelled, but the majority of the glass was intact. When Richard Sambrook asked how that could be when the blast was so huge, I replied, 'You don't think we've sat on our arses for the past few months, do you? We've been busy employing a bomb blast and ballistic protection company to replace all the outer windows with bomb film and bomb blast double-glazing.'

The glass has built-in multiple layers with air gaps running through the middle that act as a blast wave or ballistic buffer from bullets. Many people seeing a building badly damaged on the outside don't realise that the inner pane of glass has held, which means that in some cases you can still operate without being too concerned. At a staff briefing after the event Richard Sambrook congratulated us all and delivered a Churchillian address that was akin to putting two fingers up to the terrorists and demonstrating to the world it was BBC business as usual. And indeed it was, as we remained live on air with no interruption. We also managed to get some incredible footage of the explosion and its aftermath, due to quick-thinking news cameramen shooting from a safe distance in a nearby staff car park.

***

In response to Saddam Hussein's alleged weapons of mass destruction programme, the BBC was extremely concerned about this potential risk and so I developed a brand-new course on reporting from a chemical or biological and radiological (CBR) zone. To help with this I was introduced to Dave Butler, a former military warrant officer and eminent CBR specialist. His main presentation trick was to roll up and place a small ampoule containing white grainy powder on the desk of a news editor. He would then explain that if a canister containing a kilogram of the powder were to break open outdoors, the contents would scatter on the prevailing winds, killing many people and contaminating large swathes of the country. What Dave was referring to was anthrax. 'Why anthrax?' he would say. 'Well, it's simple, it costs nothing to make and if you kill one person, you frighten a million.' Many hundreds of journalists began attending the specialist CBR course in Warminster.

The BBC wanted to make a programme on the CBR terror angle and how it was being handled, or mishandled, by the police and intelligence agencies. It was time for me to meet with George Eykyn, the BBC Home Affairs correspondent, and my source, Larry. In autumn 1998, George and I began what would be three years of detailed work, gathering and pulling together information on the CBR threat to Britain, with the help of Security Service informers, and by responding to Larry's tip-offs and filming the emergency services' response to any incidents. George hoped to get up a *Panorama* programme but this was not possible. When we felt we had enough material, however, we attended a news-gathering editors' meeting to establish how we would pitch something to the public on such a sensitive subject. George kicked off with photographs and footage of our findings and openly admitted that he was struggling with how to present it. We all knew the country was woefully equipped to deal with any form of attack but we didn't want to frighten millions of viewers by getting the tone and delivery wrong. Then George had a Eureka moment: he would use footage he'd shot of a mass casualty exercise that had been run by the British Home Office. Actors, students and retired pensioners were paid to be part of a mass casualty mock-up and make-up artists were recruited to construct mock wounds and fake broken limbs, creating a scene rivalling Michael Jackson's *Thriller* video.

The next step was to hook this onto the main story, which was that the BBC had been given vital intelligence of a potential attack on one of Britain's busiest and most important airports. George carried it off with aplomb. He felt ready to take a swipe at the government and in particular the Home Office for being unprepared to respond to terror attacks. Over footage of people dropping to the floor with facial blisters, kids vomiting and sirens wailing amid confusion and chaos, George said: 'The BBC has secret access to a number of security incidents involving chemical and biological substances left at airports and railways. The question is, are we prepared enough to be able to defend ourselves?' The extended item, titled 'Is UK Prepared for a Chemical Biological Terror Attack?', featured on the BBC's flagship 10 o'clock news, which was most unusual.

At 10.30 that evening, the phones rang red hot. Some people were complaining about the graphic images shown on the news, but others were demanding we take the story to the Home Office. We had already made contact and were invited into Whitehall for a chat with a subgroup of COBR or COBRA, the Civil Contingencies Committee that is convened to handle matters of national emergency or major disruption. (COBR is the acronym for the Cabinet Office Briefing Rooms at Whitehall.) As part of our hard labour, we assisted the Ministry of Defence with a July 1999 document titled 'Defending Against the Threat from Biological and Chemical Weapons', which were considered a greater danger than nuclear weapons. We also took part in a multi-agency briefing that included representatives from the Defence Science and Technology Laboratory at Porton Down, Salisbury, and other agencies and departments in Whitehall. Also arranged was a media briefing that was addressed by the head of Special Branch.

CHAPTER 12
ON THE UP DOWN UNDER

IN EARLY 2002 Jill and I sat down one night to discuss our relationship. We'd been together for many years, and we had both been career driven but, as I can now see far more clearly, I was more absorbed by my job and everything that went with it. Quite rightly, Jill had grown tired of me being away and we both felt that we'd drifted apart. We'd tried desperately to make things work but we were running out of options to repair the damage. I still felt committed to working something out, however, and decided to go to counselling on my own.

I'll never forget my one and only session with my counsellor, Michael, a wiry man with nicotine-stained fingers and saggy clothes. His counselling room was dark and cold and had a one-bar electric fire, an armchair covered with cat hair and a huge box of Tesco's finest two-ply tissues strategically placed next to the victim ... er, client. Michael started off, in a broad Irish accent, by asking me about my relationship with my mother and father. Two hours later he ended with, 'Jesus, Mary and Joseph and all the feckin' saints, I've written enough material here for a conference. Have you never had counselling before?' I said no, only confession with Father Ahem when I was young.

I headed home that night slightly deflated as I realised I really hadn't dealt with a number of personal issues. I remembered what a counsellor I worked with at the BBC once told me, 'It's that champagne moment when you've rattled the bottle around and the emotions you can't suppress any longer go bang as the cork flies off.' In other words, trauma is layered and if you don't debrief after each layer the net effect becomes more intense and explosive. I think in my heart of hearts I knew I needed more help but my work consumed me. Later, in my own way, I learnt better to recognise the signs and with huge help from my family and friends was eventually able to move through a great deal.

In the midst of 2001, a very bad year, Jill and I had applied for Australian residency visas. Jill had told me that she and Katie were going and I had to get onboard if we were to make our relationship work. She was under huge pressure at the BBC, often working until very late dealing with staff disputes and cultural clashes. The thought of living close to her sister in Australia really appealed. I had taken some convincing: to me it felt as though we were running away from our problems.

We carried on but then in November 2002 Jill called to tell me that the visas we'd applied for had been approved; all we had to do now was undergo medicals and set a date for emigration. Jill booked all three of us in for the medical. Hers and mine were fine but then the doctor said to both of us, 'Who knows about the hole in the heart?' I looked at Jill and looked at him and said, 'A hole in the heart is when ...' but before I could finish my sentence, he said, 'No, who knows about Katie having a hole in her heart?' For a moment the world stopped spinning but the doctor then explained that though Katie would have to have more tests such as an angiogram, there was nothing to worry about. Both of us came out of the clinic thinking, 'How the hell did we miss that one?' Fortunately within

24 hours the results came back and the emigration doctor was happy that Katie was in no danger. From that moment we pinpointed the following April as the month to book flights, say our fond farewells with family and make sure we had our house up for rent.

As Christmas approached, I was called into my boss's office and told that he was making me head of high risk and occupational health and safety, which incorporated the high-risk team I'd taken five years to develop. I could see the joy on his face as he announced it, but then I slid my resignation letter across the table. He opened it, read it and dropped his glasses on the desk before saying, 'You fucking wanker.' But he quickly followed up with, 'No, Tony, I'm only kidding. I really want the best for you and Jill but I'm just gutted to see you go. I built up this position for you and it was always the place you wanted to be.' I had mixed emotions. I'd been at the BBC for what felt like a lifetime and I'd developed some incredible bonds and friendships. Also I'd just been given the promotion I'd longed for and finally, after years of giving my life to my job, I could glimpse some relief in that I'd be the boss of my own department. And I'd at last be given the funds to make a huge difference in journalism safety and provide a much better support service to those taking risks in the field. On the other hand, I was excited by the mighty challenge of starting afresh in a country that had then barely considered journalist safety, venturing out on my own without a large machine like the BBC behind me.

We enjoyed our last Christmas and said goodbye to all our family and friends and headed to Heathrow with a shed load of suitcases and a number of toys, including Polie, Katie's much loved and chewed polar bear, once white but now a sooty grey colour. My brother Jeff and his wife Sue drove us to the airport and it was only as we waited inside the terminal that I fully realised the enormity of what I was about to do. I could no longer spontaneously meet my brother at the pub in half an hour, or ask him and Sue to come around for dinner. After a drawn-out process, Sue and Jeff had not long before adopted Darren and John, and he couldn't have been happier. When I'd confessed that I was finally taking the jump and heading to Australia he had been very upset, though he understood that I needed to give it a try.

But, as was always the case with me and my brother, something funny happened at the sad moment of departure to lighten the mood. I pulled out my mobile phone and car keys and passed them over to Sue. I reached in my pocket and pulled out all my English money and gave it to Jeff. I then rummaged around in my left trouser pocket and pulled out three blank bullets and an atropine monojet injection (used as an anti-nerve gas agent) left over from the Gulf War. Jeff took one look at me and said, 'Jesus Christ, only you could do this. I suppose now I'm in for a full cavity search as soon as I leave here.' I apologised and went to give him a hug. As I placed my arm under his armpit and around his back I felt a large lump. He said, 'Bro, it's nothing. The doctor thinks it's just a sebaceous cyst.' As I found out later it wasn't a cyst, it was non-Hodgkin's lymphoma and he suffered for another four years before it took his life. I went back and forth between Australia and the UK during that period and watched helplessly as his life drained away.

After numerous chemo and radiation sessions, loss of hair, burnt soft tissue in his gut and ulcers in his mouth, he was given the news that they had found a brain tumour. I flew back from Australia yet again but this time the specialist told me Jeff was in theatre: they were going into the middle part of his brain, and it was an extremely difficult procedure. The next line was delivered in what seemed like a soft whisper, 'Tony, your brother's not going to make it. I'm pleased you're here to say goodbye to him.' When Jeff finally returned from surgery he was shocked to see me. I held his hand

and even though I told him I was here for the Liverpool match and just thought I'd drop in, he knew I wasn't telling the truth. It wasn't until a few days later that his last phase of chemo started. This nearly killed him but after umpteen tests and biopsies we were given the incredible news that the tumour had vanished and after a few days with all my family I headed back to Australia.

Jeff's illness did have a positive side. The gulf between my sister and me was still wide. It seemed to me that Angela couldn't understand why she had slogged her guts out to obtain an honours degree while, with no university education, I had cruised into a great job in the navy. We fought on a whole range of subjects. I was well travelled and I felt that she was perhaps slightly jealous of this. For many days after the brain tumour diagnosis, we watched over Jeff in hospital, still tussling over many issues, until one morning Jeff woke up and said, with a steely glare, 'Will you both give it a rest? I'm hanging onto my life here and you two do nothing but argue.' Since that day Angela and I have been close, and I believe we owe it to those strong words delivered by our brother.

It must have been no more than a few months later that Katie, who had been back to the UK, showed me a photo of her and Jeff. His face was terribly gaunt and I called Sue, who told me Jeff had refused all food and was only drinking water. She knew that his body was buckling but nothing prepared her for the morning when he collapsed on the floor and couldn't get up. Because no suitable bone marrow donor could be found, he was left with no immune system. He was put into an induced coma – I spent an hour every night on the phone to him, talking about anything and everything, knowing that the last thing to go with anyone is their hearing. He never regained consciousness, however, and the ventilator was switched off a week later. He died of multiple organ failure and septicaemia on 15 January 2008.

My 'twin' was gone. I'd lost my best mate and protector. He was larger than life, there for me whatever and wherever the situation. His wife and sons now had to fend for themselves. Jeff left a huge hole in everyone's heart that's still there today. I'd give anything for him to walk back in the door, even for just 10 minutes. Occasionally, though, I feel his spirit near me, especially when I'm in the pub.

I lost three of my closest relatives and lifelong buddies in the space of 15 years. Gerard died in 2015. As an adult, I'd crossed paths with him a few times, first in Plymouth, where he was on a training course with a roadside breakdown company. The course was all about customer service and how to answer the phone and I remember the two of us laughing at some of the calls when he stopped dead and turned to me: 'Jeez, all the private education I've had and all I am is a call centre bitch.' I saw him also in Australia as he'd emigrated there many years before me and was living a sad and lonely life. His partner, the love of his life, had left him with nothing when they split. By 2015 it was clear that Gerard's health was failing, and the drink had finally caught up with him. He was showing signs of dementia and ended up in sheltered accommodation. I had to assume power of attorney and look after his day-to-day finances. I was very sad when he died. After his funeral, which was attended by only a handful of people, I flew to the UK to give the $75,000 left to his name to his two daughters from his earlier marriage. And so another family chapter ended.

***

As I boarded that plane in April 2003, I was leaving behind a secure life, a great house in Ealing, London, a brilliant job with incredible opportunities and, most significantly, all my family and friends. The person who took this the worst was my daughter Brianna, who at 13 needed me the most. But I knew if I didn't follow Jill I couldn't see much of Katie. I felt as though I had a gun to my head.

I'd tried my best to see Brianna as often as I could, but she lived in Plymouth with her mother and her grandparents and travelling 400 kilometres each weekend proved difficult for me. For a while we met at a midway point, a McDonalds in Bristol (the Checkpoint Charlie of single parents), but with my work taking off and my new relationship with Jill, sadly the visits became fortnightly and then monthly. I really missed Brianna and though we wrote often, I felt I was letting her down by not being there during her school years. But Tracie always gave me full access throughout the school holidays and Easter and Christmas, and Brianna and I spent some incredible times together in Liverpool with my family and hiking around the Lake District. She also loved coming up to London and hanging out with me. There were always many hugs and tears whenever we said goodbye. When I knew we were going to Australia, I'd booked a holiday to Barbados, where Brianna and I caught up with friends and enjoyed the snorkelling and diving that we both loved. The time flew, but I'd desperately needed those two weeks so that I could explain what she meant to me and that I wasn't abandoning her: she could visit me any time in Australia.

When we left the UK I was in a daze, made worse by the uncertainty about my brother's health. Then, on the stopover in San Francisco I noticed a huge TV screen in one of the streets playing out a scene that could have been lifted from a movie: people were running in a field of tall grass, blood pouring from their faces and drenching their clothing and body armour as aircraft swirled overhead. I crumpled to the ground in disbelief. It was my BBC safety team, led by Craig Summers: spearheaded by veteran reporter John Simpson, BBC News was covering the Iraq invasion. I didn't know it then, but they had come under attack, by mistake, from a US aircraft, which caused untold damage.

At that point I had to let go of the idea that I was always on tap in the event of an emergency and that, for the first time in years, there would be no buzz on my pager or mobile phone. I was no longer required. But at last I would be able to concentrate on my family. Katie would become more than just someone I'd say hi and bye to; now I'd have the time to spend listening to her and praising her when she'd done something amazing.

When we touched down in Sydney, on 23 April, to a warm, sunny day, I thought I'd died and gone to heaven. There to greet us were Jill's friends Penny and Roger with whom we'd stay for the first few weeks. I'll never forget the huge fig and gum trees and the deafening sound of the cockatiels waking us up. I opened my eyes each morning thinking I'd landed in *Jurassic Park*.

***

The beginnings of the idea for my high-risk security consultancy company, ZeroRisk, had come to me when I was still with the BBC, on a very hot day in 2000 on the Israel–Lebanon border during my investigation into the death of Abed Takkoush. I'd spent four days in Beirut and Tyre talking to journalists who were covering the war when something dawned on me: they were all aware that this particular area had been heavily targeted by the Israelis, but none of this vital information had reached any of the news teams arriving in the country. This omission made them highly vulnerable to being picked off by strategically positioned Israeli tanks.

When I dug deeper, I realised it was like this the world over. On arrival in a war-torn country, journalists would simply collect their bags, hail a cab and head for the scene of the fighting, with little or no information on the risks they were about to encounter. Drivers like Abed, and others, were being badly injured or killed due to a lack of pooled security information.

As Jill and I prepared to leave for our new life Down Under, I came to see that my important risk protection work was only just beginning. At the many farewell parties that we had with colleagues, friends and family, I came to realise that I could continue the kind of work I had been doing for the BBC. Six months before I left the UK, with the help of a friend, I set up a basic website called ZeroRisk. This collated safety and security information from all the major news agencies – the BBC, ITN, CNN, Sky, ABC, APTN – represented in the News Security Operations group which I'd founded during the Balkans conflict. I had been acutely aware that all the major news networks were struggling to maintain safety and a logistical supply line in a war that raged for years and would push news-gathering operations to capacity. By pulling together representatives from all the networks we could not only share information but also pool resources such as armoured vehicles, flights, helicopters, medical assets, body armour and specialist hostile environment training. This enabled the networks to have both the best researched equipment and the most cost-effective way of maintaining a supply chain. By posting these global risks – everything from potential female attacks in certain areas in Albania to a particular junction or crossroads in Belgrade that was an accident black spot – which could be shared by the entire media community, we were making journalists and their crews that much safer.

The site could also relay logistical support information on any country listed on our Category 1 (full-blown war zone, major conflict, requiring full security and safety controls) or Category 2 database (area of political instability, riot, coup, natural disaster, requiring referral and sign-off). This information, provided by my fixers on the ground, could include safe airports and hospitals, and reliable places where you could purchase such things as food, water and fuel. Fixers are among the most important people in any news operation. Generally local to the country or area of deployment, they can speak good English and are often politically and logistically connected. They're also there to negotiate visas, money transactions and source food, fuel and shelter. I also supplied details about hiring or purchasing vital safety equipment: body armour, respirators, protective headgear and armoured vehicles. On offer, too, was safety and security training, which covered hostile environments and war zones, riots and demonstrations, chemical, biological and nuclear/radiation disasters, undercover and investigative journalism and defensive driver training with remote first aid. ZeroRisk could also provide vital security information on setting up large-scale sports and events – anything from the Olympics to the World Cup to royal weddings and funerals.

As ZeroRisk became a source that everyone could trust, I knew that I'd developed a brand of my own and I quickly registered the company as TL Risk Pty, but changed this to ZeroRisk International when I arrived in Australia. Intelligence and promulgation of risk alerts were to be the backbone and just before I left UK I was approached by Tony Naets, head of news for the European Broadcast Union, to provide such a service for his member group, which consisted of all the top European broadcasters – Deutsche Welle, ZDF, RAI and RDF. In essence Tony provided me with a paid gig that in turn meant a soft landing when I reached Australia. I will always be indebted to him for giving me this opportunity.

Initially I made Ellis Beach near Cairns my base and couldn't resist sending back to my team at the BBC a photo of myself at my computer, overlooking a sun-drenched beach, with the title 'My New Office'. I could only spend so many days, though, lounging around editing a few risk reports. I soon realised I'd have to rejoin the humdrum of Sydney and start looking for prospective clients. Although I'd always been institutionalised, having spent the best part of 25 years in the British armed forces and the BBC, I remained confident and optimistic that I could pull off this new venture.

CHAPTER 13
DEATH IN NABLUS

JUST TWO MONTHS into my new life in Australia I received a phone call from Nigel Baker, editor-in-chief of APTN in Britain, who wanted me to investigate the death of their cameraman Nazeh Darwazeh, who had been shot and killed in the Palestinian city of Nablus, on the West Bank, around 9 a.m. on 19 April 2003. 'We would be taking on the might of the IDF,' he said, 'and we need someone who's done this before. We'll require everything to be documented extremely carefully due to the legal process involved.' If I took on this job, my main fear wouldn't be coming up against the IDF, but the damage it would surely cause to my relationship with Jill. We'd only just arrived in Australia and now I was abandoning her and Katie to fly back to Europe and the Middle East on a dangerous mission with no time limit and a high chance I would be kidnapped, seriously injured or killed. But I felt I'd built up a reputation as the Mr Fix-it of security and that my presence made a difference.

I accepted the mission under my new company banner, ZeroRisk International, and arranged to fly to the UK to be briefed. I'd already put my intelligence team to work and established that Nazeh, born in 1959 into a large family, had become politically active as a teenager by joining the Popular Front for the Liberation of Palestine. This Marxist–Leninist revolutionary group, founded in 1967, was the second largest faction making up the Palestine Liberation Organisation, which was dedicated to ending Israeli occupation of the West Bank and Gaza Strip. At 17 Nazeh had formed his own splinter group, distributing leaflets and trying to recruit members. Israeli troops ordered him to leave his Nablus high school because of his activism and he was forced to spend his senior years in a nearby village. In 1979 Nazeh went to Jordan, planning to study economics. Several months after his arrival he was arrested by Jordanian intelligence and sentenced to seven and a half years in prison. I also learnt that it was easy to wipe out generations because of the way the Palestinians lived together under one roof. Destroying the entire building ensured a whole family would either be killed with one hit or be psychologically scarred forever.

There's no doubt that Nazeh had flirted with danger and death and had caught the eye of a number of the PLO hierarchy, including Yasser Arafat and Mahmoud Abbas. Having read his file, I realised I was in for a rough and dangerous ride because the Israelis had him pegged as public enemy number one. My only burning question was why he hadn't been targeted and killed much earlier. I put it down to the fact that he'd switched quickly from political activist to journalist, but apparently everyone was shocked that a family man like Nazeh – he and his wife Naela, who had a degree in literature, were parents to five children – had managed to get killed after spending more than 20 years supporting all the major news agencies in covering the Israeli–Arab conflict in dangerous settlement areas.

In London, Nigel gave me a budget for the investigation. I was to determine how Nazeh was killed and why, and to try to secure compensation for his sizeable family. Beyond following the brief and establishing the full facts of the shooting, I would need to record all my findings in our company's bank of knowledge so that they could be used to great effect in our hostile environments training courses. Ironically, investigations like this, into tragic deaths, became excellent opportunities to further enhance journalist safety and security.

While in London I met up with Issam Ikirmawi, who suggested I touch base with some of his family members in Nablus to receive a briefing before engaging with anyone else on the ground. I needed to travel on a special pass as a carpet seller so I could smuggle in £5000 cash to give to Issam's family, who could not even access, let alone afford, anything like medical supplies or much food. I was only too aware that transporting money was highly risky. If caught, I could be accused of funding Hamas, the Palestinian Sunni–Islamic fundamentalist, militant and nationalist organisation, and their terrorist activities. To avoid unwanted and aggressive questioning when entering Israel I travelled on two passports. One I kept clean (no Arab stamps); the other was an older passport with plenty of short-stay tourist stamps and nothing incriminating.

I arrived at Ben Gurion Airport near Tel Aviv late at night and did my usual trick of smoothing the way through customs by schmoozing a number of the female flight crew on the flight from London and then staying close to them, continually chatting and smiling as they walked through to the security gate. This gave me the perfect cover, as most of the airport security staff would be distracted by the women and pay no attention to me. I then elected to travel in a family taxi, which meant I'd be mixing in with the locals and wouldn't stand out by travelling on my own. After about an hour, everyone had been dropped off and I was then driven to the American Colony Hotel in Jerusalem. (I'd stayed here before while I was at the BBC and conducting background reconnaissance for an investigation into who was really behind the 1982 Sabra and

Shatila massacre, in which Lebanese forces killed between 460 and 3500 civilians, mostly Palestinians and Lebanese Shiites.) As I got out of the taxi and paid my share of the fare, I kept looking down the street to check I hadn't been followed. I would be extremely careful to keep conversations and meeting contacts down to a minimum. I knew that Mossad, Israel's national intelligence agency, had the hotel's reception, the adjacent payphones and certain doorways of guest rooms bugged. I didn't want to blow my cover this early on.

The following morning I met up with the smart and well-connected local Associated Press journalist Lefteris Pitarakis, who not only provided me with some very useful background information on the IDF's position in Nablus but also managed to secure me the passes I desperately needed to travel through Gaza and into Nablus, as both areas were still locked down and heavily patrolled and protected.

Next morning Lefteris was waiting outside the hotel in a white bulletproof Land Rover. He explained that from now on he would do all the talking and hand over all our paperwork. I was just to sit in the back and keep quiet. As we approached Gaza, you could feel a rise in tension as we saw the occasional fast-moving armoured personnel carrier (APC) with soldiers spewing out the back, cocking their weapons and firing at packs of youths fleeing into the safety of old streets and housing estates. We must have negotiated at least 12 checkpoints to reach the outer road leading to Nablus and every time we stopped we were held up by soldiers checking our paperwork, sweating profusely as they stood in the soaring heat in their heavy body armour and helmets. Finally, we came to a halt at one of the most heavily manned checkpoints I'd ever seen. It reminded me of the US fortification high up in the Mekong Delta in the movie *Apocalypse Now*. This was it, this was Nablus, and our vehicle could go no further.

I jumped out with all my kit, including carpet samples, and gave Lefteris a big hug in appreciation for all he'd done. He put his hands on my shoulders and said, 'Tony, God speed. You must be under no illusion that this is a very dangerous mission. Many people will be wanting to stop you at all costs, and if they have to kill you, they will.' The reality of my task hit me, but I was there, as always, to represent the man in the grave who could no longer speak for himself or defend his family. I needed the truth.

In so far as the hilly topography of the site would allow, Nablus was built on a Roman grid plan. This served the Palestinians, and in particular Hamas, well as it made it harder for IDF troops to move heavy armaments such as tanks and APCs around the city. For years the Israelis had battled with the locals and all the action revolved around one specific area. The Israelis would bring huge Merkava tanks through the streets. Kids would throw petrol bombs and aim slingshots at the tanks before Hamas foot soldiers fired with their shoulder-launched anti-tank missiles. Lefteris had told me that as soon as I set foot in Nablus I would be actively tracked. This statement not only made me suspect that Nazeh's killing could not have been a case of mistaken identity, but prompted me to raise my level of awareness.

Having successfully cleared the checkpoint, using my cover story that I was keen to import Middle Eastern rugs into the UK, I got a pass to drive into one of the Palestinian enclaves. I could see the magnitude of the damage inflicted by Israeli jets on villages and homes. In response, Hamas were very good at identifying and taking out anyone connected with the IDF. I went alone. Travelling at such a highly sensitive time wasn't safe but I had to take the risk.

I deliberately didn't go and see Nazeh's family first because I didn't want to get too emotionally attached: this could taint my judgement and ruin the investigation, especially if I were captured and questioned. As soon as I was on the ground in Nablus I made contact with Hassan Titi, a Palestinian cameraman who had been working for Reuters on the day the shooting took place. My job was to take statements from him and everyone who was there so I could form a picture of what had really happened.

On the Saturday Nazeh was shot, he was filming clashes that had broken out south of intersection 70, where large Palestinian crowds were protesting the death of an Al Jazeera journalist. Israeli troops had opened fire and were using tear gas and live rounds in a clash that lasted 40 minutes and injured many people. An IDF Merkava tank had slammed into the wall at the corner of an alleyway and become stranded there; everyone heard the bang. Nazeh was standing, with a group of about six other journalists, who travelled together, at the doorway of a barber's shop in the alleyway, filming the tank. He was getting great footage, but unknowingly he was also filming the events leading up to his death. Nazeh was shot in the head and died instantly.

When I discovered that this pack of journalists, from Nablus TV, AP, APTN and Reuters, had all been filming, Hassan introduced me to the camera crews who were there at the time and I quickly moved to obtain every single piece of footage I could get my hands on. Each showed various angles of the shooting but the Nablus TV camera, positioned above Nazeh's head, gave a clear view of the moment of impact. When I went through all the material, it was very clear to me the Israelis were firing on the journalists; Nazeh was not caught in IDF/Hamas crossfire.

It had been a dangerous day. I spoke to the barber, at whose doorway Nazeh and the others had been standing. He'd gone to open his shop as usual that morning when he felt something like a mosquito bite on the back of his leg. Looking down, he discovered quite a bit of blood and it was only then that he realised he'd been shot. He delivered his own basic first aid by tearing his jacket and making a bandage and Reuters photographer Abed Qusini helped him. On the second day of my stay, I went to see an elderly woman in her flat where some of the bullets had landed. She'd been making afternoon sweet breads when she heard a crack and a whistling noise. Bullets grazed the top of her head and went through her room. She showed me a scar on the side of the head and said through my interpreter, 'This is the closest I've ever been to my maker and is now a reminder of how close I came to death.'

I used news video footage and some obtained from Nazeh's own camera to prove that he was shot from behind, a 5.56 round fired from a Galil rifle. The bullet went through the back of his head. Hollywood movies show actors rolling around after a shot to the brain. In reality, when people are shot in this way, they generally drop to the ground very quickly: it's like seeing a puppet collapsing once its strings are cut. One afternoon, when I returned to the street where Nazeh was killed, I found the evidence I'd been searching for: the metal fragments of the bullet that had travelled through his brain and, buried in one of the walls, a small flechette (a tungsten steel dart, banned by the Geneva Convention, used as an anti-aircraft dart to fire at aircraft). I also found a brass shell case belonging to the gunman who had fired the fatal round. I placed it in a paper bag, not a plastic one so the DNA wouldn't sweat off in the heat. I could also see where the bullets were fired into a limestone wall. I had to get the bullet fragments out of Israel; they would become crucial evidence in any legal proceeding.

Looking again at the subpoenaed video, I could see an Israeli soldier aiming his rifle into the street at kids and camera crew. To me it was clear that he had a mandate to take just one person out, but I needed to prove this. With the okay, and the budget, from

155

Nigel Baker, who was a great supporter of improved journalist safety, I was again able to draw on the help of my ballistic forensic specialist Dave Leeming at COTEC. Dave confirmed that this was indeed a phenomenon called snapshot shooting, where a number of bullets were fired into a building to cause a distraction and then one designated soldier would take aim and fire one round – in this case into the group of journalists in the alleyway.

I had now amassed plenty of photos and video of the scene of the shooting but, of course, there was no body to inspect. So I paid a visit to a doctor in the Rafidia Hospital, who had taken possession of Nazeh's body and was saddened by his death, since he had known him for many years. I knew I was in a dangerous place: the hospital was deliberately unmarked and wounded Hamas soldiers were treated in the basement, so it was a high-value IDF target.

A tall dark-haired man who sat behind his desk in his extremely hot office, smoking a large cigar, the doctor looked like a secret agent from a James Bond film, quite expressionless, his eyes covered by reflective sunglasses. I could sense he didn't trust me and thought I was an Israeli spy. It took a lot, via my nervous translator, to convince him I wasn't and just wanted to find out what he had seen. He told me. Kids were indoctrinated into a hate programme against the Israelis. He pulled out x-rays of individual kids aged between eight and 14 with smashed bones and ripped off arms, injuries caused by flechette darts. Once one of these pierces the skin, the bone shatters, meaning amputation is the only option. He also told me that the Israelis operated a shoot to maim policy: they fired on a group of people, generally kids, so that when any were injured and taken away, the rest of the crowd would disappear.

When the doctor felt more at ease, he gave me Nazeh's x-rays. On one there was a small cross mark at the back of the skull that looked very different and remote from the large splintered bone section to the right. This was the evidence I'd been looking for as it proved beyond reasonable doubt that Nazeh was shot from behind.

After the interview, the doctor escorted me to his car; we then drove a short way and parked. As we walked together through the streets, it was like passing through a great valley of destruction, rubble and misery. The doctor, his head bowed, explained what had happened. 'My friend, the Israelis for many months flew their F16 jets over our houses at high speed and they would bomb us heavily, wiping out houses and entire generations with the press of a button.' During our walk we met some of the doctor's family and several people gave me figs and dates. I was humbled by this because they had no food.

Back at the hotel, I was visited by a number of people claiming to be friends of Nazeh and trying to harass me into revealing my information and find out what I was doing in the country. Sure that these people worked for the IDF and that at any minute I would be taken in for questioning, I continued to move around to different safe houses provided by contacts shared with me by the doctor. My life was now under threat because of what I knew. A Palestinian family gave up their basement room so I could study the evidence further. I was missing the name of the soldier who had fired the weapon, and I also needed to confirm the doctor's qualifications.

I now had the evidence that the Israelis delivered the fatal shot, because someone slipped a brown paper bag containing a VHS cassette under the front door of the house I was staying at. When I played it back, I could see the IDF soldier moving behind the tank. He was alert and watched Nazeh's position for some time, then crouched and fired the fatal shot. This matched the position and elevation created by Dave Leeming.

Back at the hospital I asked the doctor to go through the injuries again and then requested his medical credentials. I could tell by the pause before his response that we were in trouble. 'My friend, I am not a fully qualified doctor. I trained in Hungary many years ago but never formally qualified.' My heart sank: this was not good if our case was to stand up with the Israelis or even have any chance of being proved a war crime. To get around the problem, we cited him as a local clinical physician.

What made our investigation compelling and successful was the evidence we gathered under very dangerous and difficult circumstances, the forensics we conducted and the support offered to me by some extremely brave and determined individuals enduring a living hell each day just to survive and tell the world what was actually going on. But what surprised me most was the fact that those courageous locals knew of the ballistic threat posed by IDF and Hamas and had received no training in working in hostile environments or in remote first aid.

***

The following year brought a very different kind of assignment when I was approached by Scott Blakeman, head of human resources at Channel 7, which was the host broadcaster for the upcoming 2004 Olympics in Athens. He wanted ZeroRisk to head up their security operations for the games. For three months before the Olympics started ZeroRisk – well, I – represented Channel 7 at all the high-level security meetings in Athens and from those I'd provide an overall business risk report on the perceived threats, and the control measures adopted, which included the positioning by the US of Patriot missile launchers at strategic positions around certain high-risk venues. I also covered off the management of the camera and presenter schedules and recommended and drafted in the services of SWAT (special weapons and tactics) operators and senior serving people from Specialist Operations 19 (SO19), the Metropolitan Police firearms unit in London, and the Los Angeles Police Department. Every single one of them gave me 100 per cent commitment throughout. This was to be the very foundation of my company and so I needed to carefully select operatives for their vast experience, unwavering loyalty, dedication and, above all else, their sense of humour, something I insist on to this day.

ZeroRisk did its best to deliver a first-class security operational service encompassing intelligence briefings to the Seven Network executives on the potential Al-Qaeda threat on the back of 9/11, and the maritime threat. The latter was high on their radar as they'd commissioned a private yacht to be moored in Piraeus Harbour throughout the Olympics and used as a base and VIP/athlete reception and entertaining area. We had to sweep the yacht for suspect devices and assist the Hellenic Police with a clearance dive search of the hull before the vessel was allowed to enter Piraeus Harbour. We had to check it again when it was moored and two members of our team stayed on the yacht permanently to run security and vet and greet anyone coming onboard.

It was at the Olympic closing ceremony that ZeroRisk cemented its reputation. My team had covertly surveilled the movements of the executives when they were out and about in Athens. It was only as they were leaving that they learnt how we had maintained a security distance and guarded their backs throughout.

During my first few years in Australia I took on most of the work and drafted in experts as and when I needed them. I watched security companies come and go because they just didn't cut it with the clients. Some of them had extortionate office rentals to service whereas I worked from home and made the Lord Nelson pub at

The Rocks in Sydney my meeting place for colleagues and clients. Somehow it worked and the company continued to grow as word got around about our work at the Olympics.

CHAPTER 14
PAKISTAN AND AFGHANISTAN

IT WAS A cool winter's evening in Sydney in 2005 when I received a call from Phil Chetwynd, the Asia-Pacific news editor for Agence France-Presse, the oldest news network in the world, which over the years has become like family to me. He was deeply concerned about the security situation in Pakistan, where a number of western interests were being targeted for attack. The guard force in all high-risk countries is the most important security defence for any compound or office set-up. Phil felt that I would be the right person to head out and review the situation and implement the necessary security recommendations. After I put the phone down I turned to face Jill, who was standing with her arms folded and a deeply worried look on her face. She calmly pointed out that we couldn't go on like this: if I took this job then neither she nor Katie would be there when I got back.

Jill had struggled to find work when we arrived. Back in Britain she had held a very prestigious role at the BBC, but in Australia she fell foul of 'tall poppy syndrome' as HR recruiters told her that she would have to take a more junior role with less pay and work her way back up from there. Jill was, understandably, angry and annoyed and I really felt for her. We had little in the way of savings and were getting by on the money I was earning for editing a website for a European news network. Jill struggled for six months until she secured a senior HR job. I was away a good deal, and the situation was made more difficult because her closest family and friends lived in Brisbane and Perth.

The following day I called Phil back and told him that I'd take the job and would plan to be in Islamabad as soon as possible. I spent the weekend before I left trying to sell the importance of my trip to Jill, explaining that I needed to do this kind of work just until I established myself in Australia, but on Monday I slipped out of our Sydney rental and headed to the airport, just hoping that somehow everything would be alright. I'd only just boarded my flight, however, when a message popped up on my phone: 'If you're on the plane we're over and I'll be moving out with Katie.' My heart sank but there was no way I could pull out and so I reverted to my default position in any difficult personal emotional situation, getting on with the task in hand. I did try to reach out to Jill a few times once I reached Pakistan, but spent most of my time talking to Katie.

When Jill and I eventually split, she moved away and after a few months I asked her if I could move closer to make things easier for Katie's school pick-up and drop-off and activities. One night I heard a loud bang on the door and found Jill collapsed outside. When I managed to calm her down, she explained that her nephew Matt, whom we both adored, had been killed in a climbing accident in the Lake District. I'd been a favourite uncle figure to Matt and taught him to dive and climb from an early age. We were both stricken by grief and I realised that no matter what our differences were, and all the heartache we'd experienced, we could still unite in support of each another.

I've had a lasting relationship with Pakistan. The culture is amazing and the people are beautiful; they'll go out of their way to give you anything you need. On every trip I would take extra antibiotics or other personal items that were difficult to source in their land. I'd offer sweets to the kids, western magazines to the staff and scotch and wine to the office (even though this was frowned upon in a Muslim country). I was to train the Agence France-Presse security guard force in weaponry, making sure they were fully prepared for any challenge, but the main aim of my visit was to deliver a comprehensive four-day hostile environments course to all the reporters and management team.

I started my review of the guard force in Islamabad by pulling everyone together and asking them to show me all the weapons at their disposal. There was an array of very old pistols – one, a revolver with an ebony handle, looked like it had been donated by a Wild West movie production – and a number of shotguns. When I asked where their automatic weapons were – AK47s and M16s – they said that the country didn't allow them to have these. This set off alarm bells for me; against the firepower of the Taliban this poor motley crew would be slaughtered in seconds.

Then came a weapons test. Earlier that morning I'd spoken to a security contact in Islamabad, who'd organised to supply me with a 4-tonne truck and two drivers, both security trained. They parked these just off one of the side streets. Having made sure all the guards' weapons were clear of live rounds and ammunition, I signalled to the guard commander to get three of his finest ready for a major test. I checked their weapons and told them that in a minute's time a truck would appear at the very bottom of the street and they would have to deal with it. On cue, the truck roared into life, took a sharp turn onto our main street and sped towards our building. I started to count loudly, marking the seconds. The trio remained huddled together, rooted to the spot, looking at each other, wide-eyed. None of them raised their weapons and ordered the vehicle to stop; neither did they seek any form of hard cover. With the vehicle virtually on top of us, I signalled to the driver to stop and kill the engine. The three guards were visibly shaking and the guard commander was kneeling on the floor praying.

Lessons were learnt by everyone, the most fundamental that you can pay for any security guard force in Pakistan – there are thousands to choose from – but you should never judge a book by its cover. Captain Khan, the head of the contract security company, furious and deeply embarrassed that his guard force had failed, appeared that afternoon carrying a large box. Had it not been for the office manager identifying and greeting him before he could get to me, I would have been very suspicious of Captain Khan and his box and would have taken action. Parcel bombs were quite common in those days. They consisted of explosives, wiring, a battery and a trigger switch that was often attached to the flap, which would detonate when the flap was opened, either by light seeping in, a wire being pulled or when the contents of the parcel were pulled out. Attack averted, Khan, a jockey of a man with a large military-style hat, kept walking towards me. Inside the box was the most enormous cake with 'Sorry Mr Tony' written on it.

***

After the final day's training on the Friday, Phil mentioned that we'd been invited to a banquet with the French High Commission at the Marriott Hotel where I was staying. After the meal Sardar Ahmad, an AFP journalist with movie star looks, who wore suede leather jackets and sauntered around with a cigarette permanently hanging from his lip, and had been on my training course, told me that he'd cleared it with management for me to carry out a similar task with the AFP bureau and security guard force in his base, Kabul.

Reluctant to return to Sydney with no partner and child waiting for me, I jumped at the opportunity for more work in the region. I questioned how anyone could swing a visa for me, since I was supposed to be travelling the following day, but little did I realise the power and sway Sardar had with the Afghan government.

On the Saturday afternoon I was still checked in at the Marriott, which was always a major concern as it was the most attacked and bombed hotel in Pakistan. Sardar arrived, took one long look at me and said, 'You don't need to worry about such simple matters. I have contacts in high places. Don't worry, Tony, I will sort this out for you.'

At 9.30 p.m., in pitch darkness, I was told to go to a certain street at a certain time to have my visa photo taken. I was greeted by an old man who knew I was coming and pointed to a seat. I was starting to feel very uncomfortable. After all, American journalist Daniel Pearl was assassinated in Karachi in similar circumstances in 2002 and in 2001 Afghan General Ahmad Shah Massoud had also been executed by a device hidden in a journalist's camera when attending a fake press conference. The photographer was sweating and shaking, so I grabbed the photoshop owner, prompting him to quickly explain, in broken English and through gestures, that the photographer was new and had never taken a picture of a westerner. I still have the photo and the expression on my face that's saying, 'This is my last moment on earth.'

The next stop was the procurement of the actual visa. Sardar, taking drags on his cigarette, and I waited on a dark street. Moments later a police vehicle edged forward and a hand emerged. Sardar gave the hand my photograph and passport and the car drove away. In the dark and the distance we heard two gunshots. Shortly the same vehicle returned, the window came down and we recognised the Afghan ambassador, wearing a pakol, the soft, flat, rolled-up cap universally favoured by Afghan men. 'Welcome to Afghanistan,' he said, handing me my visa. After I thanked him, he continued, 'I've just missed out on some very interesting drinks and dinner and I had to shoot the lock off my door as I've lost the key. Do right by my people and look after this loveable rogue', pointing to Sardar.

I spent Saturday night sweating profusely and my stomach was in knots. At first I thought I was suffering some strange mental trauma, but it was in fact the ice cream from dinner coming back to say hello. For hours I was sick as a dog, gripping the toilet with one hand and the basin in front of me with the other. In the early morning a wave of utter dread washed over me: I had to fly to Kabul in a tiny UN plane with no toilet. Having packed my bags, I inserted a huge first field dressing up my arse, gorged on a few anti-diarrhoea tablets and headed for the taxi looking distinctly as though I'd just ridden in a horse race.

That flight was one of the worst experiences of my life. We were jam-packed into the aircraft and the smell of Jet-A fuel seemed to waft through the cabin, causing me to gag. The only reason I didn't vomit was that a woman opposite me talked non-stop and for some reason that arrested my attention. The minute we touched down in Kabul I bolted across the runway at Hamid Kazai Airport towards what looked like an old Australian dunny. I threw open the door, stood there bolt upright and, through a sea of sweat and cramp, managed to expunge the last of the ice cream. It was at this point that I noticed the heads of two Afghan boys appearing over the door. 'Mr, Mr, you play football with us, yes?'

The AFP house was situated not far from the US embassy and just a short distance from the major roundabout known as Massoud Circle. There to greet me was Coco, the AFP's office cook and cleaner, who was in his seventies. He welcomed me to Afghanistan and showed me to my room, apologising for the freezing conditions outside and telling me it would get a lot worse. I nodded and told him I'd been in Norway where we'd worked in temperatures of minus 30 degrees. Coco smiled and said, 'My friend, you are not an Arctic warrior until you have experienced an Afghan winter.' What I hadn't experienced before was being in a house where everything, floors, walls and ceilings, was tiled: it was like living in a freezer. Coco also told me to beware the dreaded hacking cough that everyone picks up from Kabul and that he put down to the cracked or blocked sewers and the amount of faecal matter discarded on the sides of the streets. I couldn't help but think that anyone with such a cough would run the risk of pneumonia. I spent many nights in my bedroom shivering uncontrollably as there was no heating and the temperature plummeted to minus 15 degrees.

Later that morning I met Daud, the driver and often lead photographer, with whom I immediately formed a very special bond. It was one of those incredible moments where you know you can trust someone with your life and many years later I was to be proven right. One of the reasons why I love working for the AFP is that no matter who you are, cook, driver or cleaner, everyone gets a chance to better themselves and the team I met in Kabul were no exception. They all did their daytime jobs but watched and studied some of the seasoned photographers and journalists as they moved around the city. Armed with this knowledge, it would only be a matter of time before they were filling those roles themselves.

This was also why Sardar had the vision to get me into Afghanistan to train their staff in how to survive in a hostile environment. I felt honoured to be chosen and within days I was in the thick of it, creating scenarios for all the AFP team to run through. One remote trauma scenario involved driving to the mountains of West Kabul. I was assured by the office manager that all the clearances had been granted, but what I didn't take into account was the deluge of snow

167

we were driving into. Before long we were becoming bogged on the top of the mountain. All the team got out and were treating the situation as if it were an exercise. After an hour in the most atrocious conditions, we freed the vehicle and were heading back down the mountain. Then I decided to stop and take everyone through a vehicle checkpoint exercise, which involves people being placed in the spread-eagled position in front of the car. Everything was going to plan until an Afghan police car arrived and held us all up at gunpoint. After much negotiation and a carton of cigarettes, we were on our way. To this day the team thinks that we planned the whole thing.

CHAPTER 15
SERIOUS AND NOT SO SERIOUS

IN 2004, THE head of SBS Television news and current affairs, Phil Martin, a lovely chap with a fearsome reputation, had a problem and had been told I was the man to fix it. For three weeks Carmela Baranowska, a tough freelance video journalist, had been embedded with the US Marine corps as they hunted down Taliban and Al-Qaeda in the remote villages of Afghanistan. She believed that the Marines were abusing local villagers and was the only journalist to return and independently cover this story. She was paving the way for awareness that, in the fog of war, people can often turn a blind eye to what's really happening on the ground. But now she'd gone AWOL in southern Afghanistan, disappeared without a trace, and Phil was beside himself with worry. I took on the task of finding her and used my extensive Afghan contacts to do just that, within six hours. Phil, impressed and grateful, offered me a contract to look after his pool of young video journalists (VJs). My first task was to introduce a risk management system, which entailed running countless hostile environments training courses, setting up a call-in system for any travelling journalists and implementing a robust hostile environment policy and country risk assessment plan.

From then on in I became the gatekeeper of safety and security for SBS and was in the very privileged position of being the first point of contact with highly sensitive and dangerous material. On my desk landed the names of interviewees, regimes, murderers, kidnappers and unseen files on high-profile political figures. The trust I built with SBS was to prove very fruitful and enduring: VJs would often call me in the dead of night, using me as a sounding board to discuss the story, how it was going and what other angles they could pursue. Mike Carey and his sidekick Geoff Parish of the SBS current affairs programme *Dateline* were grateful for this. They were often too busy to take a call or, by their own admission, just not experienced enough in risk management regarding some of the areas to which their journalists were heading.

Around this time, having separated from Jill, I started going out with a few women but these were all short-lived relationships. My focus was on being available 24/7 for SBS and my date time turned into *Dateline*. At the end of October 2004, while she was investigating allegations of police corruption in Papua New Guinea, award-winning journalist Bronwyn Adcock was arrested and had her passport taken as she tried to leave the country. A few extremely tense days followed as diplomats worked to get her passport back and we prevented her from being taken into PNG police custody by organising a friend dressed as a taxi driver to snatch her from the airport and get her to the Australian consulate.

In May 2006 the brilliant VJ David O'Shea became caught up in the violence in East Timor. Using his many contacts, he had secured the interview he'd been waiting for – with the former East Timorese military commander turned rebel leader and guerrilla fighter, Major Alfredo Reinado. He was in the middle of the interview, at Becora on the outskirts of Dili, when, as he later told the *Sydney Morning Herald*, 'all hell broke loose' as government troops and rebels fired on one another. Although we'd meticulously risk assessed this trip, nothing had prepared us for this situation.

I was dining in a Japanese restaurant in Sydney's Harris Street when I took the call from David and distinctly heard rapid and heavy gunfire in the background. Over the din I could hear him panting and trying to get some words out. I immediately told him to lie as low as possible, to get rid of his tripod as this would prevent him from running and to distance himself from his fixer, who was also part of Reinado's militia. This he did and followed my final piece of advice to travel to the top of the hill, sit tight and, when he got there, take a few photos of the area and home in on any prominent buildings or features. I then asked David to stop using his phone to file the story or talk to other journalists and friends, because his battery was running low and we needed a link in order to rescue him. My next call was to James Choi at the Department of Foreign Affairs and Trade in Canberra, to whom I explained the situation very briefly and quickly. From the photos David sent we could identify his exact position, DFAT sent a small, armoured embassy vehicle to rescue him, and an extremely difficult and dangerous situation was averted.

Ginny Stein was another brilliant VJ who graced the news offices of SBS and ABC, though she never really liked coming back to base and loved being on the road getting the story. One day, in 2007, Ginny announced that she would like to go into Zimbabwe and interview the opposition leader, Morgan Tsvangirai, who was a deep thorn in the side of Robert Mugabe's brutal regime. This was considered an extremely dangerous mission as journalists there were often hunted down, interrogated, tortured and killed. SBS news director Paul Cutler, a former head of news for TVNZ, relied on me to make the judgement whether the story was safe to take on or not. Ginny's proposal was green lit and as she started to prepare for her journey, I flew to South Africa to brief and select my team to be on standby and, if called upon, to enter Zimbabwe by whatever means necessary.

On returning to Sydney, we ran through the final plans but were stuck on a cover story for Ginny. A number of journalists had entered Zimbabwe as resource developers and for months had studied the local fauna and fungi related to water catchment areas; they even had dummy companies set up to convince the authorities that they were bona fide. As we sat in the office late one night we came up with the plan that Ginny would adopt the role of a nun: if she became compromised in Zimbabwe, she would say she was there to spread the Catholic faith and mingle with the children. This was a dangerous notion. A number of the kids she would encounter would have been recruited by the Mugabe-led Zimbabwe African National Union – Patriotic Front (ZANU–PF).

Nevertheless, in the early hours of a morning in October 2007, Ginny landed in Harare and managed to slip the security line and police gaze. We were all thrilled. We'd been made aware by our intelligence sources that the Zimbabwe authorities had now purchased a more sophisticated immigration document-checking system and she ran the risk of being flagged as a journalist on entering the country. However, she got in. But this was the start of a very harrowing 10 days as communication was patchy, though Ginny kept in touch. She would start her nightly transmission to with 'Good morning, it's Sister Soft-shoes here. The lions are very restless tonight (referring to Mugabe's henchmen) but the flock is still willing to come to the church and there are many supporters for our faith.' This meant that Tsvangirai was still keen to conduct the interview, though Ginny was then informed that he'd fled the country with his wife, Susan, to holiday in Mozambique. When they came back, she had bought the largest and most outlandish hat on the planet, which made spotting Tsvangirai that much easier. After much negotiation, Ginny arranged a time to meet and get the interview she and SBS so desperately wanted.

That night I was on edge, pacing the floor at home, just wanting to hear her voice to let me know she was safe. We also had to communicate a plan to get the small DVC cassette tapes out of the country. About 9 a.m. the following day the phone rang and it was Ginny aka Sister Soft-shoes, confirming she'd met the bishop (Tsvangirai) just before 11 and apart from a few scares with patrolling ZANU–PF, she had the interview in the bag and was heading to Mutare, close to the Zimbabwe–Mozambique border. I kept our conversation short as I didn't want her compromised at this latest stage in the game.

The next part was equally dangerous: we had to come up with a plan to get her tapes out and we did this by checking with her the best options. After much debate with Ginny, Mike and Geoff, we backed her plan to give the tapes to a trusted and former South African Special Forces soldier to walk them out. Ginny would keep copies of the tapes in her suitcase wrapped in her filthiest clothes. As she quipped to me later. 'There was no way any guard force would rummage through the contents of my bag as I hadn't washed in days.' Ginny's main concern was that she still had to get her camera out and this she secreted in a small bag secured by her feet as she was searched. This brilliant strategy worked. Ginny Stein is now based in Washington DC, where she is Radio Free Asia's managing editor for South East Asia, covering Myanmar, Cambodia, Vietnam and Laos. RFA delivers uncensored news to Asian countries whose governments prohibit access to free media.

News assignments came and went but none was quite like the night in 2011 when a number of journalists, including SBS's Brian Thompson and Amos Roberts, were under threat in Cairo as

Egypt was convulsed by the huge revolution against leader Hosni Mubarak that became known as the Arab Spring. Roberts had already been attacked by pro-Mubarak protesters but had got away and made it to a hotel near Tahrir Square. It was a frightening and vulnerable position to be in, with the armed protesters looking for and blaming foreign journalists. As Roberts would later recount, when the attacks on journalists had begun, the Australian network crews, all of whom we were protecting, had stuck together, shared information and exchanged phone numbers. They had been pegged back to the hotel and were being surrounded when Brian called me to ask what was going on and I said, 'Fuck, Brian, you should know. You're right in the thick of it.' But of course he was 20 odd floors up, facing the blind side of the square. While Brian was talking to me on the phone, I could see on TV images of the protesters piling up tyres against the hotel, ready to start a fire.

I summoned immediate assistance through a security contact of mine in Cairo, providing the names of those I needed him to get out and take to the airport. But he wasn't willing to proceed when he saw that Roberts had been named on Egyptian state TV as an Israeli spy. After much negotiating, we managed to persuade him to escort the journalists to safety in a hotel where the Australian embassy was gathering people. Through a long-time Qantas contact and friend, Grant McKay, who was running evacuation missions, we managed to get all the SBS team and the others out to safety.

**

There was some less serious work too. Thanks to my former BBC role, the ABC approached me to develop a robust production risk management system for location work. This was perfect for me: I'd been on any number of production and film sets and I was keen to build the safety framework and institute location safety training. During one of these courses, in 2006, I met executive producer Andy Nehl, who gently asked my view on what security measures would be in place for an event such as the leaders' summit in Sydney, in early September 2007, for APEC (Asia-Pacific Economic Cooperation). I explained how we'd planned for major sports and political events at the BBC. A week later I was asked to come into the ABC for a meeting with the team behind *The Chaser's War on Everything* to discuss a very sensitive production. Although I'd never seen the satirical comedy series, not being much of a TV watcher, I soon got the idea: the cast performed sketches, taking the mickey out of current social and political issues, and funny publicity stunts were often involved.

The meeting had been called to discuss ideas for a sketch to coincide with APEC – including a mock sea-borne attack. I wasted no time in telling them that this was impossible.

The police and military had been practising counter-terrorism drills in case of an amphibious assault for many months and would simply blow them out the water if they ventured anywhere near the delegation, especially with a pistol. By the time I'd finished, everyone had dropped their notepads and were slumped in disappointment at the bursting of their creative bubble. I was about to leave the room when I stopped and said, 'Wait a minute. Why not run a presidential-style cavalcade into the outer perimeter and have your boys dressed as secret agents running alongside the vehicle?' Julian was thrilled. 'Bloody brilliant! Any more ideas, Tony?' I said, 'Well, you'll have to have a comic conclusion, for safety reasons. Maybe that could be Chas Licciardello dressed as Osama Bin Laden in the vehicle, complaining about not being invited?' They loved it.

The next week I arranged for the *Chaser* team, including the production staff who doubled up as limo drivers, to receive a day's

175

training in safe driving and safe distances for the team running alongside the vehicle. I insisted that only a handful of people knew what was going on. I made sure that the risk assessment was bombproof and identified all the safety and security controls we needed to pull off such a stunt.

We were planning to go with the sketch on Saturday, 8 September, when there would be fewer people in Macquarie Street. As the due date approached, however, the team were getting restless: they were ready and wanted to go early. I was away. On 6 September I was notified that the stunt was under way, and that the *Chaser* team had got closer to the 'red zone' than anyone, including me, had believed possible.

I didn't know what to think. On one hand I was so elated by this incredibly audacious stunt but also very worried that the team might be arrested – which is exactly what happened: Morrow, Licciardello and nine other production crew members were detained and charged with entering a restricted area without special justification and their footage briefly seized. The New South Wales Police Commissioner, Andrew Scippione, was not impressed and said that the *Chaser* people had risked being shot at by snipers. What he didn't realise was that they knew they were entering the red zone when security was at its lowest and no top snipers were present.

After seven months, the charges were dropped. The ABC's lawyers had approved the stunt because they assumed that the 'motorcade', flying Canadian flags, would be halted at the first security checkpoint, but they made it through two checkpoints. Apparently most of the cops thought it was hilarious; some even asked for selfies with the team. I sent a link to some of the security guys I'd worked with around the world, including George Bush Senior's VIP detail, and they also thought it was hilarious. My old team in the UK said it was one of the funniest things they'd witnessed in decades and desperately needed after all the sadness and ill feeling since 9/11.

For me it was the start of a long relationship with *Chaser*. Another memorable scalp, in 2019, was the delivery to Vatican Square in Rome of a blimp with a cord attached bearing the message, 'Young Boys Inside/Pull Down if You Want One', which got Julian arrested again. The trick was getting ace ABC production manager Rod Oliver to get the scripts to me as early as possible and in enough time for me to laugh till my sides ached and then be able to risk assess the shit out of their ideas. I revelled in this work. It was a welcome departure from all the death and destruction I was used to in the world's hot spots.

CHAPTER 16
DESPERATELY SEEKING TONY MOKBEL

IT WAS MAY 2007 and Channel 9 senior investigator and highly acclaimed news journalist Darren Lunny, who was much too young when he died in 2022, was on the phone asking me questions. 'How well do you know Croatia, Kosovo and Bosnia? Do you have some really good security, police and military contacts there? If we gave you the name of a few people we're interested in, could you find them?' I answered, 'Very well' to question one, 'Yes' to question two and 'Maybe' to question three.

On the strength of my answers, I was invited down to Melbourne to meet with Darren and his boss. It reminded me of the BBC bar back in London where all programme deals and high-level news investigations were discussed. I was cautious with Darren initially, not really sure what I was getting into, but as we shook hands, I immediately sensed the beginnings of a deep mutual trust. Darren started asking me more questions in front of his boss, including whether I was free to work on a story with them. As soon as I'd answered in the affirmative, he pulled out a large manila file and carefully removed a series of photos and a background briefing on Tony Mokbel and his partner, Danielle McGuire. I couldn't believe what I was seeing.

Antonios Sajih Mokbel, better known as Tony, was born in Kuwait to Lebanese parents in 1965 but spent most of his life in Australia. After a tough childhood in Melbourne, he was arrested for the first time at the age of 18 and went to prison in 1992. After that he became increasingly involved in drug dealing, progressing from marijuana to amphetamines and ecstasy, and became enormously wealthy. In early 2006, while awaiting trial on drugs charges, Mokbel had learnt that the Victorian police were intending to bring a murder charge against him over two gangland killings in Melbourne. In March 2006 he skipped bail and disappeared.

I'd heard of Mokbel, of course, but asked where I fitted in. Darren, quick as a flash, said they'd been given information that Mokbel was in hiding in Croatia. Because I was extremely familiar with the area, they'd like me to start looking for any clues as to his whereabouts as they were keen to obtain an exclusive interview with him. When I queried how reliable the information and the source were, Darren said, 'Extremely.' I stressed that the stakes couldn't be higher. I might not be able to tell him, Channel 9 and the Victorian police exactly where Mokbel was, but I could sure tell them where he wasn't. All they would have to do was work back from my trail and, voilà, they should have a result.

A couple of days later I received a call from Darren saying the budget had been approved and I had 24 hours to pull my investigation team together before I flew to Zagreb. Former BBC cameraman Saša Schmidtbauer, who had an extensive database of local Croat connections, threw in his hand as an ace financial and investment investigator. I'd worked with Saša before, in the John Scofield investigation, and his larger-than-life frame backed up his larger-than-life personality and go get 'em attitude. I then contacted Jane Kokan, who had also been part of that operation, and was, in my opinion, one of the gutsiest investigative journalists I'd ever worked with. She jumped at the chance to return home.

Armed with my file, I landed in Croatia and left immediately for Dubrovnik, where I waited for the others at a stunning hillside café overlooking the harbour. As I surveyed the superyachts lined up it was obvious straight away that this was the home of the rich, famous and downright corrupt. This was my starting point: Darren had been given a tip-off that Mokbel had fled by boat, though no one knew exactly what route he'd taken.

At the stroke of noon Jane and Saša arrived. Jane gave me a warm hug and said, 'God, it's good to see you again, Loughran. You haven't changed a bit. When we finish the job, we must have a few of those large dirty martinis and one of Mum's homemade burek [filled pastries].' I looked forward to that but, as usual, insisted that no one drink while we were on the job. We had to stay focused and highly alert. One lapse of concentration could get us seriously injured, arrested or killed.

After ordering food and coffee, and checking carefully that no one was watching, I tipped the contents of my file, *Mission Impossible* style, onto the table. By the end of our meeting we all knew exactly why we were there and the challenges of the task at hand. Saša theorised that the Russians could have sponsored Mokbel's safe passage and that he could be holed up on any one of the superyachts in front us, a strange but plausible suggestion. Saša went to work on yacht dealers and harbourmasters. When he wandered over to his car he did some cursory security checks to see if anyone was overlooking or tailing him. Next, he dropped his keys and bent down to see if anything had been planted under his vehicle. He then walked right around the car to observe whether anyone had left any fingerprints: it was ZeroRisk drill to leave your car as dirty as possible for this very reason. As I watched, I was thrilled that he'd retained these skills, which I'd taught him on one of our BBC hostile environments courses.

Saša used his vast financial network to trawl through a who's who of people who just might have bought a luxury yacht in Dubrovnik, or a palatial house on any one of the Croatian islands. We all had a hunch that Mokbel might be in such a place. Jane pointed out that the tiny island of Badija was a well-known drug distribution place and gateway for drugs throughout Europe. I pulled together a small local team to run 24/7 surveillance on the fifteenth-century Franciscan monastery on the island near the town of Korčula. (Channel 9 news had been tipped off that Mokbel was living in a monastery.) Korčula was in fact the end of the infamous drug route in which heroin is shipped across Europe from Afghanistan through the southern leg of the Balkan route, mainly by road. Cocaine traditionally produced in South and Central American countries is smuggled to Croatia via sea or land from western Europe. Amphetamines and other synthetic drugs come mostly from the Netherlands and Belgium. As Jane also said, this was a drug smorgasbord that any known dealer couldn't afford to miss out on. The surveillance job was hard. We had to watch from clifftop areas overlooking the island in high heat and stay alert to every detail. Several boats came and went and after three days Marko, who was heading the surveillance team, joked that the bald and tubby Mokbel could be any one of the monks that we were observing.

Out of the blue, Saša produced a contact who was a drug informer and knew the many trade routes and players involved. We managed to get a meeting with him in Zagreb. Jane and I were keen but extremely cautious and spent a number of hours very carefully staking out the café he proposed as a meeting point. We even had people discreetly taking photos of all the occupied cars surrounding the café, which we sent to Saša for positive ID.

Our man was sitting at a table in front of the main entrance and in clear view of Saša and our team. When Jane and I arrived, he gave us a brief smile and said he didn't have much time, so we needed to get to the point. In response to our questions, he proceeded to tell us where all the main drug jump-off points were and cited Bosnia and Montenegro as places of interest. I slowly removed the folder from my backpack and placed a number of pictures of Mokbel and his associates in front of him. I watched his face for any hint of recognition and for a fleeting moment it looked as if the photos had hit home, but he pushed them back and said, 'If you want to find the rat, stay with the cheese and work your way back across Europe and to Greece. That's one of the most important pipelines for product.' I was puzzled that this man, who was way up the drug chain, would arrange to meet in full public view. This thought remained with Jane and me as we headed for Bosnia to meet the district chief of police, an encounter teed up by one of Jane's Croatian cousins, who was in the know.

The following morning the phone rang and Saša was yelling, 'Have you seen the news?' The man we'd met had been gunned down the previous evening. Saša sent me a picture and there was the informant, slumped over the table in a pool of blood with the newspaper and empty coffee cup in front of him. Jane and I were in deep shock as we ate our breakfast. Was the killing connected to our interview? Was it a sign that we shouldn't go any further? Why didn't they attack during the meeting? Saša's words rang in our ears: 'Please be very careful, my friends. Because you've been seen talking to this man, you're now considered associates.' The next few days were going to be physically and psychologically tough.

At 1 o'clock that afternoon the chief of police greeted us in an office adorned with sporting trophies, photos of him graduating from the police academy, and others depicting him standing over a gunned-down body or posing next to handcuffed gangsters with mounds of heroin bags stacked on the very table where we were seated. Jane and I recorded every word of this interview, in which we gleaned that Bosnia was facing a war on two fronts, drugs and terrorism, which, as he said, always go hand in hand. When we asked more about the terrorist angle, he mentioned that Al-Qaeda now had a base in Bosnia and was increasing its presence in Albania. I was shocked at this but even more surprised at the extent of the terror network, which had really gripped Europe. The police chief told us that Mokbel's face didn't seem familiar but gave us a contact back in Croatia that we should look up.

Once we were back in Croatia, Jane and I met up with Saša. We were all shocked about the assassination but still wanted to continue. We knew, though, that from then on we couldn't be even the slightest bit sloppy with our counter-surveillance drills and must cover our tracks, to avoid, perhaps, a potential invasion of our flat or contamination of our car. Saša also ran a third eye or counter-surveillance team on us.

The police chief's contact came good and we met him in a large park café just outside Zagreb. He was a tall, fit man who had once been a senior officer in Croatia's elite special forces but since the war's end had moved around in the underworld. In fact, he was more use to the criminals than most people since he'd seen that the end of the war was in sight and had confiscated and hidden a huge arsenal of weapons ready to trade on the black market. As Jane and I questioned him, he moved and shifted in his seat until Jane said, 'You look very nervous. Do you think I'm a Bosnian Serb?' He retorted, 'Well, it had crossed my mind.' When Jane asked, 'Do you have a problem with Bosnian Serbs?', he said, 'Not at all. We buried these people many years ago, and that is in the past.' I then chipped in: 'And maybe you can tell us where you buried them. A lot of the authorities would like to know.' He smiled at me and said, 'We're sipping coffee right on top of a few of them.' Speechless, I stared at Jane in horror and disbelief. By the end of our interview, it became clear to me that Mokbel was not among us but somewhere along the Balkan drug route. Just before we got up to move away, our contact mentioned that Greece would be a great place to focus attention on – there were many networks in existence, one of which was people smuggling.

We spent two months talking to all our contacts in Croatia and Bosnia and ruled out the possibility of Mokbel being there. We did, however, uncover some remarkable gangland information, and during the investigation I contacted Larry in London to inform him that there was a possibility Mokbel was being protected by the Russians. I was then instructed to take a number of photographs of Russian oligarch superyachts in Dubrovnik and surrounding areas and send the images back to Britain.

The sad thing was that, in all our time on the ground, the clues were there and everyone we spoke to indicated that if you wanted to get truly lost, then the Mediterranean was the place to do it. We had strong indications that Mokbel might be in Cyprus or Greece and this hunch proved correct: he was arrested by Greek police in Athens on 5 June 2007, after giving vital clues to his whereabouts when a phone call he made to Australia was intercepted. We provided Channel 9, and no doubt the Victorian police, with useful evidence of where Mokbel wasn't, even though they were given a warm lead. Channel 9 secured an interview with Mokbel in his cell in Athens before, in May 2008, he was extradited to Australia, where he is still in prison.

CHAPTER 17
BAD TIMES

IT WAS A hard year, 2014. After the investigation into Sardar's death, and my own near-death experience, I was invited into the Reuters compound to obtain an insight into their security measures. To my surprise, they had no visible armed protection. Their view was: 'We don't want weapons lying around and we have enough time to get out.' At the top of the hill behind their compound was the shell of an old T52 tank left there by the Russians. Behind this was a swimming pool with a beautiful view of the dust bowl of Kabul. This was never used by the locals because it had a sinister past: the Taliban had used it for executions.

I was offered a drink and there, on the coffee table, was a photographic book about Afghanistan that just blew me away. It was the work of the very talented Anja Niedringhaus, the only woman among the 11 Associated Press photographers who had won the 2005 Pulitzer Prize in Breaking News Photography for their work in Iraq. She was there and I was able to talk to her. By her own admission she was addicted to Afghanistan and Iraq, with their high level of danger and uncertainty. She was compelled to go back into these high-risk areas time and time again. 'The story of Afghanistan really captured me.' When I asked her to name the hardest and riskiest photo she'd taken, she gave a huge smile and said, 'Why, the 100-metre finish line shot, as you only get once chance.' And there was I thinking that it would be a close-up of a Taliban or a Peshmerga fighter.

I never saw her again. On 4 April she was killed while covering the 2014 Afghan presidential elections. The attack took place at a checkpoint on the outskirts of Khost. While Anja and her AP colleague, Canadian journalist Kathy Gannon, were waiting in their vehicle, an Afghan police unit commander walked up and opened fire, yelling, 'Allahu akbar' (God is great), and killing Anja and severely injuring Kathy. Found guilty of wounding, murder and treason, he was sentenced to death. Sometimes you encounter someone very briefly but form a bond. There was great mutual respect when Anja and I met for that one and only night in Kabul. We laughed and joked and felt lucky we could chat freely over contraband gin in the Palace of All Palaces, as they called the news organisations office just below Kabul Hill, and the famous Taliban swimming pool.

***

No one will ever forget what happened when a lone gunman, Man Haron Monis, entered the Lindt Café in the APA Building in central Sydney's Martin Place at 8.30 a.m. on 15 December 2014 and at 9.45 took 10 customers and eight employees hostage. I'd just returned from a run about 10 a.m. when I was contacted by a Channel 7 producer informing me that they thought there was a hostage siege under way in Martin Place. She couldn't give me specifics but said it was pandemonium in the newsroom and she would call me back with more detail. As I waited I tuned in to Channel 7 and saw the location of the siege, directly opposite the Seven News studios. The producer called back again and asked if I was free to come and join the team in Martin Place and stay on air with them: they needed a subject matter expert who could talk them through everything that was going on. I had first-hand experience in this as I'd covered many terror stories with the BBC, particularly the Stansted hijacking in February 2000. I quickly pulled together my go bag of spare shirt and trousers, underwear and sleeping bag, jumped on my motorbike and headed into the city.

I made the location in record time. Anchor Chris Reason told me immediately that it looked like an Islamic State attack and hold-up, but after grabbing a phone and studying the images of the flag that the hostages had been forced to hold up to a window, I said immediately, 'It's not IS.' I knew what it was: the black standard, an old symbolic flag I'd often seen in Syria, Iraq and other areas of Arabic Middle East. I also explained that if it were IS we wouldn't be in a siege or stand-off position but more likely conducting a body count and filming a public beheading. Chris looked at me and started to change the notes for his next segment.

It was at that point that I asked him why he'd been tipped out of the Channel 7 building: surely they would have had the exclusive, being right on top of the Lindt Café. Chris told me that the police had evacuated the Channel 7 building but had used the office to set up surveillance and sniper positions. I pointed out to Chris that not long after I and the ZeroRisk team had finished our stint at the Athens Olympics, the Channel 7 executive had asked the building management team what protection staff would have in the Martin Place studio area for their *Sunrise* programme. Their concern, quite rightly, was that the line-up for the following day was often trailed or promoted the night before with the future guests, including Prime Minister John Howard, sitting on the couch in the studio with their backs to the large plate-glass windows – sitting ducks for everyone from angry protesters to high-level terror groups. To make matters worse, everything was at street level, with little or no security. The huge floor-to-ceiling glass panes were the only thing stopping an attack on the studio staff and any special guests.

Not long after a brief discussion with building management, I'd received a call from one of the senior security staff asking me to come in and take a look at the problem. I'd already been in the studios so had a good idea about the extent of the glass. It wasn't dissimilar to the problem we'd faced and solved at the BBC and which greatly limited the damage caused by the 2001 IRA bomb attack. It was clear that the panes of glass installed in Martin Place were not explosive or ballistic rated. I produced a report on what Channel 7 needed to do to rectify this position, a job that would take time and money. Having been given the green light, I then worked very closely with a protective glass specialist company and even conducted a series of bomb blast and bullet penetration trials.

Once I'd outlined this to Chris, he made two phone calls, one to his boss and one to building management. He then managed to get back into the building, entering in relative safety from the rear, and took up a gallery position overlooking the Lindt Café. We'd literally secured him the best seat in the house and Seven News began with some incredible wide and close shots of the event. However, Chris wasn't granted free rolling access, since with all incidents like this the police place a blackout on filming such sensitive events as police tactics and potential terror actions and atrocities.

With Chris rolling into the main live feeds, I was asked to support Mel Doyle, who I highly rate as a journalist and is a very lovely, warm person. During the chaos I fed her information on what should be going on behind the scenes. No sooner had I gone live for Channel 7 than my phone rang red hot and BBC World TV and Radio, CH News Asia and TVNZ all wanted me to contribute to their live bulletins. I pulled in one of my team to offer depth to our service and we kept this going right through the afternoon. Three hostages escaped about 3.30 p.m. and another two just before 5 p.m. There was a tragic ending to the siege just after 2 a.m. on 16 December as Monis fired at six hostages who were running from the building. A few minutes later he shot towards the kitchen and the hidden police listening device installed during the night picked up the sound of him reloading his shotgun. Another hostage made it out the front door, and then police Tactical Operations Unit teams were ordered to slowly move in. Then Monis shot café manager Tori Johnson fatally in the back of the head. Police stormed the café and killed Monis, but fragments that ricocheted from the many rounds fired by a police officer ended Katrina Dawson's life. Three other hostages and a police officer were injured by police gunfire during the raid. Police declared the siege over soon after.

The morning after the event I stood in the background, watching with interest how the police would handle the press pack. Although the end of the siege was only hours old, it was clear to everyone that the police had made some glaring errors The journalists, mostly very young, bombarded New South Wales Police Deputy Commissioner Catherine Burn with a number of sensitive questions. I expected such pertinent enquiries as why the hostages died, why the police didn't go in earlier, why negotiations failed, how many shots were fired and why the commando units and SAS didn't get involved as they regularly did in countries like Afghanistan. After a good 15 minutes, however, none of these materialised. I can't help but think that if the journalists had been more seasoned, the session would have been different.

A joint federal–state review released in February 2015 focused on Monis but did not cover the actions taken by police during the siege. Those troubling aspects were covered by an inquest conducted by the State Coroner, Magistrate Michael Barnes, which began at the end of January 2015. In May 2016, while the inquest was still being held, I took part in a 9NEWS special, fronted by Karl Stevanovic, called *Inside the Siege: The Lindt Tapes*. I suggested that although the police had been right to be cautious about what might have been in Monis' backpack, suspected at the time to contain a suicide bomb, I questioned the rescuers' choice of high-velocity 5.56-millimetre rounds, shrapnel from which killed Katrina Dawson. As I pointed out, such rounds skip quite hard and will ricochet, causing terrible damage to the human body. I asked why they didn't use dum-dum – hollow-point or soft-point bullet – rounds.

I reached the same conclusion as the almost 600-page Barnes report, which was released on 24 May 2017. There had been a failure in comprehensive risk assessment, and the communication from hostage to police had been extremely patchy: no fewer than eight calls made by the hostages to the negotiators had not been answered. As well as the ammunition for the siege being the wrong type, there had been heavy use of such distraction devices as smoke and stun grenades. I was saddened to learn this. I knew, and know, that the police have an unenviable and dangerous task in confronting such highly dangerous situations. However, being acutely aware of the commando and SAS approach and experience, I felt the baton should have been handed over to them much earlier. It is worth noting, too, that most of the journalists who were close to the danger that day hadn't received any high-risk hostile environment training.

***

I often say on our hostile environment training courses that when you work in dangerous places you don't have to go looking for trouble, it will come to you. At the beginning of July 2016 I was pulling together a team to assist a news organisation with a story about an alleged paedophile ring in the Philippines, when my phone rang. It was Tracie Walker from retail giant Kmart, asking me if I had heard about the attack on a café in the Bangladesh capital of Dhaka. I did, of course, know what had happened. On the night of Friday, 1 July, about 9.20 p.m. local time, five young militants had entered the Holey Artisan Bakery in the well-to-do Dhaka suburb of Gulshan Thana, a stone's throw from the Australian embassy. Armed with assault rifles and machetes, they had opened fire and taken diners hostage at gunpoint. People had been shot or hacked to death. Twenty hostages had lost their lives: nine Italians, seven Japanese, three locals and an Indian.

The rescue operation, named Operation Thunderbolt, began about 7.40 a.m. on the Saturday morning. Among those involved were the police, members of the Bangladeshi armed forces, the paramilitary force called the Bangladesh Border Guards and the Rapid Action Battalion (RAB), an elite anti-crime and anti-terrorism unit of the Bangladesh Police. Thirteen hostages were rescued but two police officers lost their lives and 25 were injured, as were a number of civilians. Although Islamic State claimed responsibility, Bangladesh believed Jamaat-ul-Mujahideen Bangladesh, an outlawed home-grown Islamist group, was behind the attack. In the past it had conducted low-level attacks but lacked the capacity and resources to stage the big assaults, which were generally carried out by Al-Qaeda or IS. The seven men sentenced to death for their involvement in the bakery bombing were accused of being members of the JMB.

Tracie was concerned about locals and Kmart team members in Dhaka. I took my grab bag, passport, medical kit and a few thousand dollars in cash with me and arrived at Tracie's office in Melbourne mid-afternoon. I told her I would get to Bangladesh immediately and ensure her people were safe. My flights into Dhaka were already booked and Jamie Ross, my chief of staff, had already briefed me fully. I'd worked with Jamie, who was formerly Royal Protection and Police Special Operations (SO19), over the years and always admired his high level of professionalism, his extensive contact list and his fierce loyalty to his job. He came onboard full time in 2016. He has incredible military and police connections around the world and can be credited with producing the global specialist team I have today.

When I arrived in Dhaka on the morning of 2 July, the airport was in chaos as westerners fled town, fearing that they were going to be targeted and killed. I was met by two close colleagues, Sharmin and Shafiq, local Bangladeshis whom I'd trained and worked with. (I had had to create a new identity for one as he was top of Al-Qaeda's attack list.) After exchanging our usual brotherly warm greetings, we got into a battered Datsun Cherry, driven by Shafiq's old friend Abhoy, whose name means fearless. A mountain of a guy squashed into his seat, he had his usual expressionless gaze but I knew him to be incredibly loyal. Down to his right I noticed the usual array of defence weapons: knife, club and small baseball bat. With a simple but reassuring nod in the rear-view mirror, he sped us off to our accommodation in one of Shafiq's friend's compounds. As I looked around, I could see that life for the Dhaka locals was going on uninterrupted; a terror attack would not stop their need to scratch out a living and provide vital food for hungry bellies.

My first visit was to the site of the attack. From what I could make out, most of the counter-terror heads had not seen this coming and were left shocked and deeply embarrassed. After all, Bangladesh's economy is propped up by expats investing in a variety of infrastructure. But I was there to represent the retail world: Bangladesh was and still is one of the main exporters of finished linen and cotton products. My concern, though, as always, was not the damage the attack had done to the retail industry but to the people – the office workers whose livelihood depended on a regular income, the driver who was saving enough money to put his children through basic schooling, the cleaner who had extortionate medical bills to pay for her parents' hospital stay. I knew that Tracie felt the same and our similar vision would be much needed as I was about to deliver the harsh message that life in Bangladesh would not be the same again.

My meetings came thick and fast. I received a top-level brief from a number of high-ranking officers in the military and the police, who promised that their reaction to this attack would be brutal and swift. And they didn't fail to deliver: during the first few weeks of my visit no fewer than 1500 people were rounded up and interrogated. Convictions were then levelled at the network supporting the attackers. For some time, confusion reigned as to who had actually carried out the attack. Islamic State claimed responsibility but most fingers were pointing to Jamaat-ul-Mujahideen Bangladesh.

It became abundantly clear to me that any retail client wanting to continue in Bangladesh would have to build business resilience. After returning to Australia and presenting my observations and findings to Tracie and MD Guy Russo, I spent the best part of six months going back and forth to carry out everything from selecting and redesigning a new HQ to training drivers in evasive driving techniques. Our work was extensive and relentless and drew on all my previous military expertise and experience. I was then able to apply all this knowledge to redesign the security protection for all new commercial buildings and operations throughout Asia. Based on the success of our hostile environment training, I reshaped a course to cater for business travellers and rolled this out to all of our retail clients in the area. Kmart also engaged me to provide a business risk analysis of what happened and how their international sourcing services could be protected.

* * *

Ever since ZeroRisk was formed, we had delivered a risk insurance protection service for major global clients but our business expanded hugely after the Holey Artisan café attack. We began to encourage companies to spend time, money and effort trying to avoid incidents that might require a security, medical evacuation or expensive insurance response. It took me a while to convince them that we were offering something different: they relied on signing an insurance policy at the end of each year and, as a safe bet, engaged the same medical evacuation company. I departed from this model and based my service first and foremost on security risk assessments, like the one I did for Kmart, that would minimise incident, injury and death in any place on the globe where a company was prepared to invest or visit.

CHAPTER 18
ESCAPING THE TALIBAN

UNDER THE TALIBAN, investigative and network journalists were regularly detained, robbed and shot. That's why I was employed to train news networks in how to deal with kidnapping and detention scenarios. The Taliban were ruthless. Shah Marai, who came from an area north of Kabul, had worked for Agence France-Presse since 1996; since 2002 he had been the agency's chief photographer in Afghanistan. On 30 April 2018 he rushed to report a bomb attack outside the Presidential Palace in Kabul – one of two suicide bombings by IS that day – and was caught up in a secondary blast from an explosive device. The power of the explosion propelled him and his camera nearly 2.5 metres into the air and his back was broken as he fell onto a concrete security fence. He was unceremoniously placed on top of other casualties on a flatbed truck to be taken to a hospital, only to be pronounced dead on arrival. When I heard of this, I felt so sad. Marai was such a lovely man with a huge heart. He left behind six children.

I remembered Massoud Hossaini, AFP photographer and Pulitzer Prize winner, showing me a photo of a number of blast victims piled high on a truck being transported to hospital. He had been filming when a suicide bomber detonated a bomb in a Shiite sanctuary in

Kabul where 80 people were killed and 150 badly injured. Massoud told me that through his camera lens he could see a person's fingers moving: he was obviously dying due to the weight of others on top of him. The image haunts Massoud to this day. Footage of previous bomb blasts showed police and locals dealing with the aftermath in the same way: load all the casualties onto a single truck and race off. No first aid was ever given and by the time the casualties reached hospital they'd either bled out, were suffering from hypovolaemic shock (where severe blood loss makes the heart unable to pump enough blood to the body and leads to organ failure) or had died from positional asphyxia. Something needed to be done.

Once again, I flew into Kabul to review the situation, pay my respects to Marai and his family and offer comfort and support to the AFP bureau staff. My job now entailed reviewing how news teams were rushing to report on events. Whenever there's a bomb or terror attack in Afghanistan the police close the area down very quickly and often the news teams are left inside the cordon, which is extremely dangerous. All such cordons are the targets of secondary attacks that can come in the form of an explosive device being planted in a nearby taxi, car or inside the metal tubes of a bicycle, of which there are thousands.

We created ambulances out of the staff vehicles and insisted that a medically trained driver stay within eyeline of the journalist, ready to lend assistance. We taught everyone how to deliver advanced medical assistance in the field, such as applying a tourniquet under pressure in a fast-moving vehicle. We taught them the importance of getting life-saving fluids into somebody to ensure any chance of survival, and we did this by teaching advanced cannulation, which is inserting a small needle in the vein of an arm or leg and introducing fluids such as plasma expanders directly into the blood. They learnt the procedure to adopt following a bomb blast so news networks knew what to do. They learnt to get into the mindset of the would-be bomber and determine where an explosive device might be planted. They also learnt what could offer them the best form of protection, such as walls, ditches and trees. As I left Kabul I felt a sense of achievement and worth. Marai's death was a tragedy but it had not been in vain.

***

I knew things were bad when I heard, in August 2021, that the Taliban had taken over the outlying areas of Afghanistan. Word had spread of some of the assistance I had given journalists and NGOs (non-governmental organisations) over the years and now they were reaching out for vital help. But such a mission was going to be very tricky as I also knew that some of those calling for help didn't even have passports. I made it clear from the start that, though very well connected, I didn't belong to any news networks and that I'd be giving my time and support voluntarily. More importantly, as I emphasised to the journalists at the very beginning, I couldn't guarantee a visa or entry into any other country. My mission was to get them out safely to Doha in Qatar. A lot of countries promised visas but many failed to deliver and some humanitarian emergency visas were used just to get people out of Afghanistan and be processed in Doha. They never guaranteed them entry into the country issuing the visa. Even if the Afghan people were to flee on a humanitarian visa, it would not, sadly, guarantee work.

In truth they really didn't care where help came from. The Taliban were bearing down on them and they were desperate. In those earlier days I heard some very harrowing stories and was sent video clips from Basim, one of my evacuees, of Taliban going house to house to find anyone associated with journalists or NGOs and pulling them out to be beaten. Another journalist sent a clip showing the Taliban in the north executing a number of people and letting their bodies fall into a ready-made grave.

Ahmad had worked as a journalist and interpreter in Kandahar for the Americans and had also carried out undercover investigations for a number of news agencies. One of these, into the Taliban's IED tactics, placed him top of their death list. He contacted me out of the blue via WhatsApp: 'I've heard you can get people out. Please please help me. The Taliban have found out my address and have said that I'm a spy and will be executed.' He was going to try getting out via Spin Boldak, in the southern Kandahar province of Afghanistan, near the Pakistan border, but considered it too risky. He was now heading to Kabul to go into hiding.

My security contact in Kabul made a couple of calls to gauge the Taliban advance, as did my other contact and very dear, brave friend, AFP journalist Aamar Wakil. His grandfather, Coco, whom I had met in 2005, had been through a lot of Afghan wars and used to ride his bicycle 10 kilometres from the edge of Kabul to get to work with us through the coldest winters. Both contacts were from very respectful families, wonderful people I'd worked with for years and who always treated me like a brother. They rallied around their own contacts within the Taliban, mainly in the media liaison areas for the north/central and southern districts. This time it was really dangerous. Like most news agencies, AFP were pulling back to France and had rehearsed their evacuation plan weeks before. Aamar, who was staying behind to continue filming for AFP, remained as cool as could be.

I began to see the picture of desperation emerging as thousands queued by the airport gates in a last-ditch attempt to be accepted for a flight to freedom. The women and children first mentality did not prevail: the American, British and Australian embassies shut up shop on 13 August and positioned themselves in the now heavily guarded and fortified Hamid Karzai International Airport. The lifeboats had been cut adrift and it was every Afghan local for himself or herself. As the list of journalists and NGOs requiring evacuation grew longer, embassy staff were nowhere to be seen and remained incommunicado throughout. I had a list of 15 people, including young mothers and their babies, so I continued day and night to try and figure out what the evacuation system was, who was running it and what was the best way of getting these frantic and desperate people onto a list.

A CBS News security colleague called me on the 24th saying, 'No one is getting out, we're finding it really hard, your evacuees won't be at the top of the list. Give me the names and we'll submit them but I'd suggest you seek other ways out.' When I heard this, I felt a cold shudder run through my body. I'd put all my faith in the CBS-coordinated evacuation plan but now I needed to initiate multiple plans to get my evacuees out of Afghanistan. Having just one plan would be suicide. When push came to shove, Australia, Britain and the US were no help, despite me sending a video clip of Taliban going around from house to house looking for my evacuees. It was appalling.

The Taliban had originally given the Americans three months to get out of Afghanistan but reneged on this and marched on Kabul within two weeks. They now owned all the roads in and out of the city and those leading to the airport. People were looking nervously at the geopolitical situation and moving from the provinces to Kabul. The situation was risky and uncertain. I'd spent a solid 48 hours calling anyone I thought could help. Shocking images still swirl through my mind of desperate Afghans hemmed in outside the airport wall, some with the right paperwork to leave, being crushed and often beaten by the Taliban and Afghan police.

I appeared on SBS News, pleading with the Australian government, and in particular the Department of Foreign Affairs and Trade, to do more and to come out of hiding from within the airport. I pleaded for them to lend vital assistance to Afghans with Australian visas. This fell on deaf ears and to this day no one has ever been held accountable for failing those who needed them most in their darkest hours. I wasn't alone in my request. The ABC's head of investigations and current affairs, Jo Puccini, had one family who'd already been issued Australian visas. Even though they ran the gauntlet of injury and death at the airport every night, they were constantly ignored and left to fend for themselves in an extremely perilous position.

At approximately 11.30 Australian time on 26 August 2021, the situation got much worse: an IS affiliate in Khorasan Province detonated a suicide bomb at a gate to the airport, killing an estimated 170 Afghan civilians and 13 members of the United States military. We at ZeroRisk had predicted something like this: it was too good an opportunity for any terror organisation to pass up. It was the intelligence that this attack would happen that forced me into recommending our evacuees to stay at home while we explored safer options.

As one day morphed into the next, I drew on every contact I could think of, prioritising them into different categories: private airlines, billionaire businessmen, heads of international news networks and journalist agencies. I would call and email them all, persisting until I got a result, then call and call again, call and call again. At one point, my partner, Kylie, looked at me and said, 'Will this ever end? You haven't had a decent sleep in days.' She understood, though, how deeply passionate I was about the Afghan people and the great affection I had for them.

One day I was given the contact details for the head of the Ministry of Foreign Affairs in Qatar. I wasted no time and was put in touch with a wonderful woman called Sara Abdulla Al Saad. She instructed me to send a letter to Sheikh Mohammed bin Abdulrahman Al-Thani, then deputy prime minister and foreign minister of Qatar, requesting assistance for 15 people and asking that they be added to the Qatari flight evacuation manifesto. I heard nothing for a while, then received acknowledgement that my evacuees had been added to the list. Another few days passed and I was starting to look at alternative exit plans, via the Uzbekistan–Pakistan border, but this was considered too dangerous as the Taliban had sealed off entry and exit borders into Afghanistan.

Then I received a message from a number of sources that the Qataris were running evacuation missions from the Serena Hotel and anyone on the lists would be accepted. I'd already set up a 24-hour communication link via our ZeroRisk security app, SecApp, and WhatsApp and sent out a message instructing my 15 people to get to the hotel for processing. Immediately, Ahmad messaged me back and told me that he'd got through and was sitting in the lounge of the hotel and that his name was on the list. I told him to check the other names from the WhatsApp group on the list. Yes, the names were there. I posted an urgent WhatsApp message instructing all the others to get to the Serena Hotel as soon as possible.

Ahmad, tired and physically depleted from his journey from Kandahar and days spent in hiding, stepped up to the task and began to coordinate everyone on our list. One person wasn't on the list and it took all Ahmad's negotiation skills to convince the Qataris that they were family. Ahmad placed his life on the line for this United States-bound family and, in my opinion, it was incumbent on the US to grant Ahmad a special immigration visa. As far as I know, however, this never happened.

A call came via Andy Bolt, our US security chief, that an American lawyer named James Smith was requesting assistance for one of his military friends. The man's Afghan military interpreter had fled during the US pull-out but had left his wife Sapna and two-year-old son Ibrahim behind. James was concerned because Sapna had been going down to the airport wall every night, waving her passport and US visa at the military outside, but had been beaten, trampled on and whipped. Immediately I requested James get Sapna to download our SecApp. She came up on our tracker and I was able to guide her to the Serena Hotel and had a room booked for her and Ibrahim. Ahmad made contact with her at the hotel and protected her all the way to flight check-in and stayed with her throughout.

The next problem we had was communicating with all the evacuees on the bus during their transit through at least four Taliban checkpoints en route to the airport. Because it was dark and the bus windows were blacked out, everyone was concerned that they didn't know what part of the journey they were on. I instructed them to monitor their SecApp and sent messages alerting them to exactly were they where. At 2 a.m. (Kabul time) I announced to them all that, according to their track pin on my SecApp map, they were inside the inner perimeter of the airport. The WhatsApp messages came in thick and fast. Ahmad posted, 'Thank you respected Mr Tony I will never forget your help and assistance.'

***

On 10 September 2021 I received a WhatsApp message from Taib Naqibullah, who had been working for many years for the US Afghan women's mission, to which the Taliban were vehemently opposed, and was a member of the Afghan Independent Journalists' Association. He had been given my details by Jane Worthington from the International Federation of Journalists in Sydney. She was being inundated with Afghan and Pakistani journalists desperate to leave Afghanistan and felt that we could assist Taib because he was high on the Taliban's wanted list and in grave danger of capture, torture and execution. Taib was caught in a tricky situation. He'd gone to the US embassy in Kabul to hand over his passport as he was getting a special immigration visa because of his work. Taib was, though, caught short by just one day, as the Taliban entered Kabul. He was forced to flee without his and his family's passports. He tried to make contact with the US State Department but no one returned his call. In desperation, Taib was turning to me for advice and assistance.

When I first established contact, I was struck me by his intelligence and his extremely calm, rational and caring manner. Without passports, he had to stay with his family and move around to avoid arrest and detention. To make matters worse, the harsh Afghanistan winter was now setting in. I turned to Brendon Hempel from ZeroRisk's aviation support, Stratos Group. He and I had worked together in the past and he was our go-to guy when any of our company missions required it. These usually involved pulling someone out of some Godforsaken hole following a gun battle in the dead of night. I explained my dilemma and Brendon agreed that he might have a chance of getting one of his planes based in Dubai into Mazār-e Sharīf, which was about three hours north of Kabul. I contacted Taib and explained that he should head north to Mazār, a 426-kilometre road journey through Taliban checkpoints. But before he set off he downloaded our SecApp and we tracked him along the way. When he got to Mazār, the Taliban had taken complete control of the airport and so we moved him on to the Uzbekistan–Afghanistan border, were he stayed in hiding until our arranged safe evacuation.

In the meantime, I called the US embassy in Tashkent, the Uzbek capital, every day and explained Taib's situation and forwarded all his paperwork. I then spent the week trying to secure the right contacts in the US State Department and was sent down a dead-end path every single time. On 15 December I actually called the US ambassador's house in Tashkent, explaining our situation, pointing out that all it would take was for someone to travel to the Afghan border, walk across the Friendship Bridge over the Amu Darya River, which connected the northern Afghan town of Hairatan with Termez in Uzbekistan, and instruct the Taliban to let Taib and his family across. It was so simple, and after all, Taib had the right special immigration visa. But all I got was a flat refusal.

Because they had no passports and no chance of evacuation, I instructed the Taib family to return to Kabul, stay in hiding and ride out the winter. In the meantime I contacted a pilot friend of mine in the US who has some very influential contacts in the State Department, but they would not help. I called him again in January 2022 and this time he connected me directly with a senior representative of the department. After running through Taib's case again, they confirmed that his details had been entered on the next Qatari/US list. Finally we had breakthrough and I could inform a deliriously happy Taib. After a few weeks' wait, he and his family were finally put on an evacuation flight from Kabul on 30 March and arrived in the US-sponsored camp in Doha. He sent me a video message and this email: 'Thank you very much for all your assistance and continued support and every follow up on my file. Without your support I may not be able to get here. I am extremely thankful for the support of each and everyone of you and in particular Mr Tony Loughran who closely followed my case and helped me so much at every stage. Thank you sir. I can't express myself how to thank you for this assistance and support.'

As far as we're concerned his case is closed, but thousands are still open. These are the people who sacrificed everything to support the west in its fight against the Taliban and other ruthless terror networks. The battle to free them should not stop here.

CHAPTER 19
FOR THE PLANET

FOR ME, RISK stretches beyond people, particularly in war-ravaged and dangerous places; our planet is perilously at risk, and I've been involved in some amazing environmental projects. The first had its beginnings back in the incredibly hot summer of 2009 when three shark attacks in Sydney Harbour in two weeks led to widespread panic and caused the cancellation of the Manly Wharf Bridge to Beach ocean paddle. On 11 February, a naval diver on an exercise was attacked by a bull shark and lost a hand and a leg. The next day, a surfer off Bondi Beach had his left hand nearly severed by a great white. (His hand was reattached but later had to be amputated.) The third victim, on 1 March, was a 15-year-old boy whose leg was badly lacerated while he was surfing with his dad at Avalon Beach. I knew this victim well as I lived in the area and it happened on the morning I and four friends were diving nearby.

In response to this surge in attacks, the New South Wales government asked a specialist team, led by marine biologists and shark experts, Dr Amy Smoothey, Professor Vic Peddemors and CSIRO marine researcher Barry Bruce, to investigate. Their study was to be the most comprehensive and technologically advanced of its kind ever undertaken in Australia. The focus would be on the three species of shark most associated with attacks on humans – great whites, tiger sharks and bull sharks. The aim was to discover how sharks used Sydney Harbour, if they favoured particular areas in the harbour and to consider whether humans and sharks could co-exist in these waters. The team would need to capture 25 bull sharks that would then be fitted with internal tags so they could be tracked by an extensive underwater surveillance system.

I heard about the project in 2011, just after I'd just finished a very intense trip to Afghanistan, when I received a call from my good friend, dive specialist Pete Talbot. I'd worked with Pete on a number of dive jobs for the ABC *Catalyst* science programme and we'd always had a great time doing what we love best: being in the ocean among some spectacular marine life. On all of these jobs I was the one commissioning Pete; on this occasion, he was returning the favour. He explained that he'd had a very unusual and interesting week's worth of diving booked with a good friend, Rory McGuinness, but had just realised he'd double booked: 'Any chance you can step in?' I listened intently as Pete explained that the dive job was for an independent TV production about the shark study, commissioned by the ABC and to be called *Shark Harbour*.

Now he had my undevoted attention. I loved shark diving but even in my work for BBC's *Blue Planet* had never had the privilege of diving with great whites or bull sharks. Pete went on to explain that the job title was assistant to director of underwater photography. When I asked what this entailed, he just laughed and said, 'You'll find out when you meet Rory.' I gave him a provisional yes, then set about researching Rory McGuinness. His CV blew me away and I was soon reminded by others that this man was the Australian Neptune. He'd worked with the most prestigious marine conservation specialists and was renowned for his wonderful cinematography and minute attention to detail. I was both overwhelmed and inspired by the thought of working alongside such a person.

When the day came for me to visit Rory at his camera workshop in Artarmon, my jaw dropped as I walked into a vast warehouse that contained just about every camera, lighting and sound rig you might care to mention. As I rounded a corner, I spotted a battered and dirty door that led to Rory's private cave. I knocked and after a booming headmaster-like response of 'Enter', walked in to see Rory standing there, lean, mean and with a hint of 'Who the hell are you?' in his eyes. My usual confident stance gave way to a stuttered introduction as I explained. Rory stood still for a minute and said, 'Well, you look fit enough to be my DOP. All I have to do is give you the safety briefing.' He then picked up the biggest sound pole I've ever seen and said, 'Simple job, Tony. All you need to do is dive around me as I'm working the camera in the water and just jab the shark with this pole if it gets too close. Jab, jab, jab – just like that.' It was at this point that I started to understand the gravity of what I was getting myself into: in fact I was just there as a 'shark bait' insurance policy. Rory smiled as he watched me jabbing with the pole. 'Great job, Tony, and it'll be much better when we're in the water.'

Having covered off several other matters, Rory felt relaxed enough to explain to me some of his gadgets he'd invented over the years. One really caught my eye. It was his very own underwater camera housing made out of a large lump of dense Perspex, but when you got closer you realised the extent of the engineering involved. There were little pistons to push inside the housing onto the main camera buttons and even a tiny nipple to which you could attach an inflator hose. This hose was used to pump air in or bleed air out when the camera and housing were in the water, thus allowing you to maintain neutral buoyancy with such a heavy object. The next gadget that intrigued me was a small torpedo-shaped Iconix camera, which was tough and durable and, when submerged, would offer a fish-eye lens shot of the ocean and the surface. The only thing you had to remember when using this was how it went into the water: if you got it wrong the image would be inverted. The next most important thing was not to get it too far into the shark's mouth.

I left Rory's studio brimming with excitement and confidence. He'd been a delight to meet and I was really looking forward to working with him. I would remain glued to him throughout the project and soon came to liken him to the underwater equivalent of a bomb disposal expert, cool, calm and collected.

Because of the nature of the shoot, and the need to cover every angle with saturated footage, I called upon my other friend and great work colleague, ex-Royal Australian Navy clearance diver Tim Hayes, who knew Pete well and was super keen to join the team. Tim is the guy you need on board for any remote shoot as he can save the day by making modifications to broken kit, or go that extra yard when everyone else is failing. We'd worked on some amazing ocean projects.

The day we set off from Sydney I couldn't help but think of those scenes in the movie *Jaws* were everyone heads out on a beautifully sunny morning from an idyllic town brimming with happy people. Tim and I, and shortly afterwards Rory, arrived at the Port Stephens boatyard, north of Newcastle, in good time, parked both vehicles and proceeded to unload all of our dive and film kit onto the jetty. A few minutes later we were greeted by the team from New South Wales Maritime, who helped us to get everything onto our boat. After a short safety briefing we headed out around the point to a well-known diving spot off nearby Stockton Beach.

Our mission was to document the number of sharks that swam through this area and to investigate why there hadn't been more attacks, given this was a stopping off point for great whites as they headed south to colder waters and winter hibernation. Wasting no time, we set up the trailing line from the back of the boat and Rory began loading his camera into his purpose-built housing unit. After a few technical adjustments, and a white balance and lens check on the camera, I was just about turn to Tim to give him the thumbs-up when I noticed that the housing had bits missing around the lens cover. Thinking something was wrong, I stopped the camera being lowered into the sea and pointed out the problem to Rory. He just smiled. 'See this chunk here? That was a tiger shark up in the Northern Territory. I couldn't shake him off – he just kept coming back at me, biting hard on the front of my camera, and in the end I just flicked him off with my flippers. This other bite here was from a mean-looking hammerhead. That one got very close.'

For the first few dives I sat topside as they reeled in shark after shark; I can remember counting five sharks in one day from the same spot. The first few days were glorious, with stunning weather and crystal-clear visibility. It wasn't glorious, though, for very jet-lagged producer Ed Radford, who flew in from the UK and arrived on the second day. He started to feel very queasy as we bobbed up and down in a small vessel with the smell of chopped mackerel wafting from the chum barrel we were using as bait to catch the sharks. Ed really suffered and at times was delirious. Because we wanted the money shot of the shark swimming onto the mackerel, opening its jaws right up, Tim and I came up with the idea of running a second line out to the shark and attaching the Iconix housing to the line just behind the hooked bait. The only problem was we forgot to tell Ed what we were up to and he decided to pop his head under the black monitor hood that we used to view the underwater images. Suddenly there was an almighty yell. Ed had popped his head into the hood just when a 3.5-metre shark opened its jaws to take the bait, creating the impression that it was about to pull Ed right into its mouth. We all howled with laughter but also knew that we had something very special to offer the documentary. Poor Ed, wiped out with jet lag, seasickness and now shark trauma, had to take a few hours out.

We spent five days catching, tagging and returning many great whites back into the deep ocean. Tim and I helped Rory by hopping into the water, freeing the line from the Iconix camera, or steadying the shot as the shark was released from its cradle and getting the vital image of the shark gliding past and heading for safety. The days were long: we had to dive, film and edit from 7 a.m. until 9 p.m. We then had to clean and prepare our dive kit and cameras for the following day and so we barely had a chance to eat. This was par for the course, though, when filming in the wild.

One day, as we finished a major interview with New South Wales Maritime, it became clear that we were missing a great part of the story: we didn't have any footage of the pinger sonar, the small pod that sat deep in the water and would store valuable data as each tagged shark swam by. If this proved successful, Maritime were considering having a signal receiver station at each surf lifesaving station at every beach. The idea was that when a tagged shark broke the surface it would send a warning ping to the station, which could then evacuate the beaches.

Rory said that we would have one opportunity to pick up this shot up and we would be freediving – no protective cage, no armour suit – for about 50 minutes. When he looked at me and asked if I was up for it, I replied, 'Damn right I am, Rory.' Without flinching or hesitating, we kitted up. This time Rory was diving on a rebreather scuba set, which meant there were no bubbles and the fish and sharks would get closer, which is exactly what he wanted.

I was kitted out with a number of GoPro cameras to get additional shots for cutaway shots, a dive slate (an erasable sheet or board on which you can write) and undertaker pen, and that long safety pole I had practised with so often at Rory's place back in Sydney. I had one last buddy check from Tim on the boat, then slid quietly into the water. I found Rory dead ahead of me, completely weighted down and sitting at the bottom of the ocean. He wanted to be in negative buoyancy in order to pull the camera back and get the shot he needed when the recording device came down off the boat. My eyes were fully open as I felt quite nervous about my environment. A cacophony of sounds around me was punctuated by the hiss and bubble of my own slow breathing through my regulator. With my right hand I gave Rory the diver's signal, 'Are you okay?', and received an affirmative. With a slight pump of air into our buoyancy vests, we were off into a deep trench. All was going well until we hit the biggest plankton bloom (or green algae) water I'd ever experienced.

This wasn't good. Visibility dropped to 5 metres at best and at our depth of 25 metres I started to lose focus on our position. Rory continued to film as we waited for the Maritime support boat to position itself directly above us and then for me to let Rory know that they were just about to drop the sonar recording device, which was weighted down by a large piece of old tank track. On the first attempt, it descended much too quickly for Rory to get his shot and he signalled for me to go again. I gave a few tugs on our safety line to the surface, which alerted them to the fact that we ready for the second drop. It needed a third go to achieve the right effect.

This filming sequence went on for quite some time and we had only a few bars of air left in our tanks when I heard an almighty bang in the water. At first, I thought the boat had been hit but then I turned to my right and glimpsed a large grey shadow disappearing in front of me. I kept my eyes fixed on the shape, then swivelled my body left and right and up and down to give myself a better chance of seeing the shark. Conscious that I felt we were being buzzed – i.e. the shark was getting closer and closer each time – I wrote on my dive slate, 'Did you hear the bang? Do you see what I'm seeing?' Rory, unruffled as usual, wrote back, 'All good, just a few more shots and close-ups and we're done.' The time ticked by and seemed like an eternity, but we finally finished. However, the tricky part was yet to come as we had to stay at 4 metres for seven minutes, close to the surface in a plankton bloom with sharks circling, to conduct our decompression stop. (This is what prevents the bends.)

At last my dive computer beeped to tell me that it was time to return to the surface and I let out a huge sigh of relief as I boarded the boat and rerigged. This was my last day. As I drove back to Sydney, after such intense work in some very dangerous positions, my body was unconsciously swaying and rocking in the car.

***

That same year, 2011, I was just about to head out the door when I heard the question, 'Excuse me, mate, but are you Tony Loughran?' Always on the alert and conscious of security, I said, 'No, but you should try next door. What do you want with him?' The guy, who turned out to be a very gutsy and driven insurance and aviation nut named Jeremy Rowsell, had flown across the Pacific in a single-engine light aircraft with legendary pilot Jim Hazelton, as Charles Kingsford Smith and Charles Ulm had done, for the first time, in 1928. The aim was to raise awareness and money for the Royal Flying Doctor service. Jeremy and Jim took off from Oakland International Airport on 7 April, then crossed the Pacific, making stopovers at Hilo in Hawaii, Kiribati (Christmas Island), US Samoa, the Fijian capital of Suva, Norfolk Island and Brisbane before reaching Sydney. As Jeremy noted at the launch of their adventure, which he called Flying 4 the Doctors, Kingsford Smith made his historic flight in the same year that the Royal Flying Doctor Service first took to the air from Cloncurry in Queensland.

The amount of plastic waste on the beaches of small islands and the giant gyres of plastic particles in the world's oceans had become the catalyst for On Wings of Waste (OWOW), using plastic to power flight. Jeremy's next ambition was to fly from Sydney to London in 2012, on what would be the first ever flight using fuel made from blended plastic. He described it in his publicity as 'a classic barnstorming adventure flying at low altitudes of 5000 feet in a single-engine plane'. But Jeremy wanted to know how to survive if the inevitable happened.

Just as he was finishing his spiel, Jeremy said, 'You're Tony, aren't you?' I confessed that I was and that ZeroRisk was my company. 'Now let's find a decent bar – I've got a mouth as dry as Gandhi's flip-flop.' We then spent a good few hours talking. I greatly admired his drive and zest for life and when he finally got down to asking me if I could run a sea survival and critical decision-making course for him I was happy to agree.

The dates for the sea survival were set and I drew on my contacts to organise a day's session in an aircraft/helicopter escape tank. (Helicopter underwater escape or egress training prepares passengers and crew for an emergency evacuation if an aircraft crash lands on water.) I took a number of GoPros and filmed Jeremy trying to escape many times from a mechanical simulator that spun and twisted before slamming into the water in the tank. The idea is to stay calm, figure out which way you've ended up – head up or down in the water – and then unbuckle and make your safe ascent to the surface. That sounds pretty easy but when they make the cab and tank dark, and introduce noise, it requires a whole new skill level to escape.

With this course under his belt, I informed Jeremy that within the next 12 months we were going to 'kidnap' him, and he wouldn't know where or when this would. Sure enough, four months later we found out from his work that he was coming back to Sydney from Chicago after clinching a major insurance deal. He would be tired but heading in to the *Sydney Morning Herald* to discuss a cause very close to his heart, the plastic that was filling the oceans. We immediately called a few friends at the *Herald* and told them what we were up to and so the stage was set. As Jeremy entered the underground car park, we hit him with a number of flash bang pyros, fired a few blank rounds off from our AKs, gagged him, put a hood over his head, bound his hands and bundled him into my Pajero. We filmed all of this as we were creating a TV documentary about his journey.

We then drove him 20 kilometres to a spot in the wilderness and pulled him out; by this stage he was sweating and heaving for air. We slowly removed the masking tape from his mouth, cut his plastic ties and gently took off his blacked-out goggles and pulled the bag off his head. More or less nose to nose with him, I said that he had 10 minutes to turn on the GPS I'd given him. He had to be a checkpoint down the river plotted on the GPS by 10 p.m. and it was now growing dark and getting quite cold.

For the next two days, with little sleep and many challenges, we ran him ragged and into the ground, and yet he came back for more. The challenges he had to face included negotiating an armed checkpoint, skinning and preparing a rabbit, kayaking to a bay just before the open ocean, conducting a night dive with me and my team and planting a dummy explosive under a jetty in shark-patrolled Pittwater. The last challenge was to sit in a one-man life raft for six hours overnight. He managed this with aplomb but in our final debrief admitted that he needed to get better at informing others about his plans or mission statements. Then he went home exhausted.

Jeremy's Sydney to London plan did not pan out, due to problems with timing, logistics and fuel, but another great plan came together when my good friend, former BBC natural history producer Jo Ruxton, visited Sydney to deliver a speech. I decided to catch up with her for dinner and drinks and invited Jeremy to attend. He and Jo hit it off immediately and Jeremy came up with the brilliant idea that if we could get hold of the then brand-new fuel derived from plastic waste, we could fly a small plane from Sydney to Melbourne to demonstrate the potential for plastic to power aircraft. We all left the pub that night buzzing with what we could achieve. When Plastic Energy, a company in the forefront of the growing sector involved with converting end-of-plastic to fuel and oil, came on board, I knew we could achieve our aim.

Jo went to work explaining our project to her lifelong friend and colleague, Sir David Attenborough, and Jeremy flew to meet the great man at his house in London. He was delighted with what we were planning. Jeremy had also made contact with Plastic Energy and managed to secure a 50-litre barrel of the newly processed fuel, which he had shipped from Spain. Then he and ace aviation specialist and lifelong friend Chris Clark got to work on filtering and diluting this smelly sticky sludge ready to decant into five large drums, which someone had to take across Australia. I put my hand up for the job and invited Jo to come across and accompany me on a five-day road trip from Sydney to Perth, dropping the barrels off at strategic airports. The journey was tough but we had some laughs, especially on the night, in one particularly rough town, when we checked into a motel and, much to the shock of the young receptionist, I took the last barrel of fuel into my hotel room for safekeeping. Throughout the trip we filmed and conducted many radio interviews for the project.

On 2 February 2017 the pioneering flight began: Jeremy and Chris took off in Jeremy's plane and I took off with another veteran pilot in his light aircraft, which was the safety/tracker plane. It was a glorious moment at Illawarra airport, near Wollongong, as we taxied behind Jeremy's Vans RV-9A two-seater and watched it splutter and roar into life before darting straight off just under the clouds and levelling out along the coast. We followed suit and I had the enormous privilege of taking the stick part of the way along the magnificent coastline into our first fuel stop.

We were making good time and the engine was extremely responsive and didn't miss a beat. We were creating history. All the political wrangling and import regulatory stresses we had endured disappeared in that one 15-hour flight. The first phase of our mission was coming to an end: we'd proven that using conventional fuel blended with 10 per cent fuel manufactured from plastic waste worked. In the words of Plastic Energy, 'Jeremy in his Vans aircraft RV-9A proved that end-of-life plastic waste can be transformed from a pollutant into a viable alternative jet A1 fuel and can also be used for any diesel engine.' After a fabulous welcome in Melbourne we checked into our hotel and wasted no time in downing some of the finest champagne and attending a great dinner before heading to a local bar and continuing to celebrate.

This was a story about how one man's idea became a magnetic pull for a special team and changed the way we look at our fragile planet. As Sir David said to Jeremy, 'The On Wings of Waste flight will, I hope, bring attention of the world to this great solution, which is there waiting to be taken if only we can get the support.'

***

That statement by Sir David Attenborough got us thinking. Jeremy, Jo and I, and OWOW, of which I was now part, had so much more to give. We were in a unique position to leverage off the back of our plastic flight success to do more about the plastic ocean problem. But it wasn't until I met Tim Pearce, the general manager of M Resources, a metals and mining company and one of our clients, that I realised we were missing one of Australia's major problems. Australia had been exporting its end-of-life plastic to China for processing, but China no longer had the technology or the capacity to do this and informed Australia that it didn't want any more plastic. And not only had China stopped collecting Australia's plastic garbage but for years it had been burying its collected recycled waste. I was shocked to discover this and thought immediately that some of our mining clients, always considered dirty polluters, were in a great position to offer advice and assistance.

At a meeting with Tim and clean fuel guru Duncan Mackenzie, we realised that there were plenty of mines not being used in Queensland which had the capacity to store end-of-life plastic. It was feasible that we could build an end-of-life plastic processing plant in Gladstone, a large seaport off far north Queensland that already had the infrastructure to deal with high volumes of all types of plastic. It also had large running conveyor belts that could transport the plastic from tankers in the port to the processing plant. In addition, here was a cut-price solution to use diesel derived from end-of-life plastic to fuel the large mining machinery trucks used in the vast coal fields in Queensland. With all this information under my belt, I reported back to Jeremy and Jo and sold them on the idea that this was the way to go and that what Gladstone also needed was a Marine Environment Education Centre because ending the scourge of plastic had to begin with educating young people.

My first visit to Heron Island also made me realise the importance of addressing the plastic ocean problem. It's a coral cay – an island formed from reef sediments – that sits at the southern point of the Great Barrier Reef and 80 kilometres north-east of Gladstone; the ferry ride takes two hours. This made me think about this amazing place as an extension of the environmental message.

Sir David Attenborough, who first visited the Great Barrier Reef in 1957, considers Heron Island one of his all-time favourite dive spots. He returned in 2015 to film another documentary about this extraordinary ecosystem. I have been fortunate to visit the island on many occasions with family and friends, and the crystal-clear water and stunning marine life have me coming back for more. I remember one magical night under a clear starry sky lying perfectly still next to my daughter Erin and son Tom as we watched a large loggerhead turtle slowly make its way past us. We were so close to this beautiful creature, and stared in awe as it built its chamber, laid the most amazing silky white eggs and then buried them under a mound of sand. We must have lain there for quite a few hours, and it was only when we were trying to extract ourselves very quietly and slowly, with no light but the moon, that we realised that many other turtles were also making their way up from the shoreline for the same purpose.

Having been so close to these stunning creatures, and others such as sleek black-tipped reef sharks, made me think that this is what children should be doing, and not burying themselves in their phones or laptops. That's why I strongly believe in building an education centre at Gladstone so kids can not only see the problem we have with contaminating our oceans but also have a better overview of what we're doing to protect it. In conjunction with this, I want kids to spend time on the island. This is surely worth fighting for: we owe it to our children and their children, and their children's children. As I write, these ideas for Gladstone are still in the pipeline and we are also exploring hydrogen energy sources.

Jo Ruxton received an MBE for her work in marine conservation, and is the co-founder of Plastic Oceans Foundation, which works tirelessly to educate the world about the importance of clean oceans.

CHAPTER 20
LEARNING THE LESSONS

WHEN THE PHONE rings at 11 p.m. I can predict that the desperate voice on the line, often from a news agency, is going to ask me one or more of the following questions: Do you have a person who can translate for us on the ground in Ukraine (or wherever)? Do you have a car we can book for our news crew? Do you have a security person we can use and how much per day? Do you have people trained in first aid? Do you have any flak jackets? Does it really matter where you get them from?

To me, such queries spell disaster: they all reveal that no preparation or thought has gone into sending news crews into the hell that is a war zone. A number of news agencies still ponder whether they should even cover such events. It seems incredible in this day and age, when the world's biggest news stories are taking place, that people in authority are still second-guessing how to send their correspondents into hostile situations.

War is bloody, shitty and downright nasty and it doesn't discriminate. If you're going to cover it as a journalist employed by a news agency, or as a freelancer, there's no room for hesitation. Planning and preparation for war coverage should be done well in advance of news crews hitting the ground. To do nothing is not only negligent but a huge breach of a company's duty of care. When I worked in the military, I was shocked at the sight of the world's press teams, obsessed with getting a story, running headfirst into extreme danger while those of us trained for these situations were trying to get out or find effective cover.

And it's still happening. As the terrible story of Russia's invasion of Ukraine started to unfold in February 2022, the major news networks like BBC, Sky and CNN were pre-positioning themselves in Kyiv, Lviv and Mariupol, waiting for a continued Russian offensive. But between 24 February and 2 April, six journalists were killed. The first was 50-year-old Brent Renaud, an acclaimed American filmmaker and freelance journalist who travelled to some of the darkest and most dangerous corners of the world to produce documentaries that transported his audiences to lesser-known places and highlighted the suffering of their people. Renaud, who was gathering material for a report about refugees, and photographer Juan Arredondo, who is an adjunct professor at the Columbia University Graduate School of Journalism, were travelling in a vehicle towards a checkpoint at Irpin, a suburb of the capital, Kyiv, when both were shot at by Russian forces. Arredondo was injured in the lower back but Renaud was shot fatally in the head.

Early reports suggested that he was working for the *Times* in Ukraine because he was found with a press badge from the newspaper that had been issued for an assignment years before. This piece of information caught my eye. During my time at the BBC we were often concerned about staff ID cards not being returned on the expiration of a contract and being found on individuals who had used them to gain access to meetings or navigate their way through checkpoints. This caused major confusion when anyone was injured or killed and the person was attributed to the wrong network.

Renaud was one of the most respected independent producers of his era, according to Christof Putzel, a filmmaker and close friend. 'He was just the absolute best war journalist that I know. This is a guy who literally went to every conflict zone.' Let's analyse that statement for a minute. Renaud was the best war zone journalist because he got the shots and produced some of the most amazing documentaries – fact. He was also a calculated risk taker, and had to be, to get the footage he needed – fact. So you have to ask yourself, 'If I'm going to be the best there is, surely I need the best support on offer?' Throughout the many investigations I've conducted into the deaths of journalists, I've learnt it doesn't matter how old or experienced you are, there's always one element in life that will catch you out or trip you up.

I've spent most of my life trying to protect journalists like Brent Renaud but also many other people who must work or travel overseas in challenging and dangerous places. I've also investigated incidents and attacks that have destroyed lives, so that such events won't be repeated. In the end, it's all about risks – taking them, as I have so often, whether during my time in the military, as head of safety at the BBC or in the company I founded – and minimising them to prevent injury and death. Risks are sometimes necessary, but they can also provide, as they have often have for me, a way out of difficult personal situations – better a flight to Bangladesh or Afghanistan than facing a tough discussion with your partner.

Not one job is the same and because ZeroRisk has lived on reputation, we generally pick up work from direct cold call contact. This can either be through calling us direct or via our website. Any one of my team will take the call but they generally refer it back to me or my client relationship manager. Every call is logged and then prioritised and the right person for the job allocated. The choice will be down to such aspects as age, gender, ethnicity, experience and personality. Because we now cut across so many sectors – media, retail, government, mining, education, expeditions and more – it's crucial to get the right person on the right job and ensure the comfort and trust of the client. Over the years I've expanded my team, carefully recruiting a highly skilled cadre of safety, security and health professionals. They can not only provide high-level protection on the ground but give specialist training in the classroom to journalists and travelling business executives.

Our headquarters are in Sydney's Northern Beaches but we have an extensive global footprint that offers sunup to sundown security and health response and protection anywhere in the world. And our work relies on some pretty advanced technology. There's the SecApp, which provides the one-stop shop security and health alert and information service our clients had been asking for. It contains an emergency help function for when they're seeking assistance, a check-in function to let everyone know they're okay, a 24/7 security Live Alert system which is plotted on our SecApp dashboard and a list of all vetted hospitals, hotels, embassies and airports. Also on the app are a list of security training videos and information, video advice on any security situation, a personal travel form that can be downloaded, completed and used in an emergency, 24/7 tracking (every 10 minutes) of an individual's phone and something we call Telemed, which allows a client to dial into a ZeroRisk GP anywhere in the world. There's also Travel Docs, which updates a traveller's flight itinerary with all the latest security and health alerts and allows company managers and supervisors to see where anyone is around the globe at any one time. It also gives more contact information on that person, such as hotel, visa type or any changes to flight details.

We also get involved in corporate fraud investigations – determining where a company has seepage or financial drainage due to embezzlement or syndicate manipulation of procurement systems. In 2020, for example, I was called to investigate the authenticity of a woman who publicly donated a huge amount of money at a charity event. During the course of two months and a great deal of surveillance and undercover work, we established she was a fraud and was out to destroy the director of the company holding the event because he'd recently spurned her advances.

We hunt down missing persons, such as criminals on the run, but also, more in line with our preferred work, we look for people who have disappeared off the face of the earth due to mental illness or depression. This work is really rewarding: it's so moving and satisfying to see the faces of family when they are reunited with their loved ones.

***

The hostile environments training I inaugurated at the BBC remains a significant part of my work today. Since then, I've delivered numerous courses in many hotspots around the world for many high-risk companies. Today the course covers more than 14 subjects over a period of five days. I spend the first four days teaching all the subject matter by running the attendees through some very realistic scenarios. Day 5 is then spent consolidating all the lessons taught and running through a test that puts the delegates under an enormous amount of pressure. This allows us to test their critical decision-making and how they work overall as a team.

By the time the course finishes everyone is exhausted and drained. Some have said to me, 'I've realised over the past five days that working in hostile and high-risk areas isn't for me. I'm returning to my desk and letting others get on with this work.' Others like Shamsa Ahmed have stated that the lessons they learnt were vital for their survival when faced with dangerous situations. Some have even said our training was so real that it proved a life-changing experience. Many journalists who have covered Bosnia, Chechnya, Kosovo, Afghanistan, Iraq and Ukraine owe their lives to what they've been taught.

Let me give you a taste of the first couple of days. After the participants meet at 8.30 a.m., in an extraordinary cacophony of conversation and a surge of excitement, the first lecture begins with me writing the words 'complacency' and 'curiosity' on the white board to remind everyone that from now on those two words are the ones they must immediately recall when going into any situation. I then ensure all delegates have downloaded our SecApp and just as the last person has done so, I signal for one of my team, who's pretending to be a journalist and course participant, to keel over on the floor while crunching on a blood capsule and vomiting profusely. The vomit is in fact a mouthful of chicken soup and always manages to make its mark on the poor delegate next to him. By this stage everyone is usually just sitting there, or perhaps standing and looking, with no one even moving to lend assistance. I let the whole situation play out; everything is videoed and played back immediately. And I always replay the video at the end of the course. After being exposed to an abundance of risk assessment and incident response skills, they all cringe when they see what was recorded on the first day.

On Day 1, too, I cover planning and preparation, which is generally an explanation of the protective equipment people need to take into the field. This can range from something as simple as ensuring that your clothing is the correct type and colour. Khaki or black, for instance, indicates a combatant. As all my years of experience have taught me, it's how you're perceived and how you look that draws unwanted attention and attack from the military and police. However, something too light in colour will have you lit up like a Christmas tree in any field environment. The other thing I stress is how you can be seen or heard at night when you're in the field.

I also give a lecture about weapons and explosives and then one on first aid, straight after covering off bullet wounds and blast injuries: you have to understand how to minimise risk, and how to respond, when everything has gone terribly wrong. The only change to this style of running order is the kidnap scenario, which comes before teaching people about situational awareness, self-defence and conflict resolution. Many years ago the actors we used as armed kidnappers were set upon and immobilised by the delegates, who were pumped after learning about self-defence.

Straight after dinner at the end of the first day I line everyone up outside and have them all spread out at 3-metre intervals in the pitch-black darkness. I give each delegate a pair of binoculars, a pad and a pen. Then over a 40-minute period a number of my instructors generate a light or a noise that must be identified. We have scratching of clothing, cocking of a weapon, a cigarette being lit, cologne being liberally applied, eating from a metal tin, the red light on a camera and a call coming in from a mobile phone. Most people identify approximately 70 per cent of the noises and lights, but experienced journalists achieve around 80 per cent because their senses are so much more acute.

Only a handful, however, have ever got the sniper that we've dug in and completely camouflaged a couple of metres in front of them. The great reveal is completed by the sniper firing a single shot 5 metres away, much to their shock and bewilderment. This lesson is vital. In my experience, journalists can be guilty of looking into the distance and not above them or at what's directly in front of them. I learnt a harsh lesson during my military days when, more than once, I stumbled across what the military call a command wire. This is a red and black electrical cable, one end of which is attached to a roadside bomb and the other to a power pack with an operator ready to turn or press a switch that sends an electrical current down to the bomb and bye bye soldier.

My favourite time to trigger the kidnap scenario is when the delegates have been on the go all day and are getting tired. I dim the lights and play a very lively video of a gun battle before signalling all the members of my team to hit every door of the classroom and fire off a couple of blank rounds before slamming all the delegates to the floor. In the middle of this I have a number of people shouting and screaming, and a dog handler with a large German shepherd making its presence known. One by one each delegate is bound, gagged and blindfolded and thrown up against the wall, with their head well and truly planted on the brickwork and their legs spread wide apart. We then check that no one is so distressed that they want to pull out of the exercise. I make no excuses for crafting this scenario: course members need to know exactly how it feels and what they should be doing to cope with this traumatic 'dislocation of expectation'. As I explain to them afterwards, 'While there is silence there is hope.' Silence generally means that the people taking you captive are organised and professional and won't panic and draw attention to themselves. It is during this silent phase that one of the instructors collects and bags all the delegates' possessions – watches, wallets, money, ID cards, even condoms. This phase is often known as back to zero because it's a classic capture technique whereby you are returned to nothing, and this is when you feel most vulnerable.

Next comes a stark reality check delivered by people who are mostly former military and know how to defend themselves. They're also holding real AK47s, though modified to fire blanks. Slowly but surely, over a period of no more than two hours, the delegates are taken into a darkened room one by one and made to sit crouched down in front of an interrogator. The journalists then have to stick to their cover story and not put themselves or others at risk. Following the briefest of interrogations, they're thrown back in the room and against the wall. After their two hours are up, we slowly remove blindfolds, gags and ligatures, look at each person and quietly ask them if they're okay. When everyone has been processed we all sit around in a semi-circle. Some are talking loudly, some are laughing, some are crying, some are just gazing at the wall. The relief is palpable and we spend at least an hour running through the debrief and giving them tips on how they can handle such situations better in the future.

Day 2 is generally dedicated to the subject of checkpoints and ambushes. As most experienced journalists will testify, the ambush is one of the scariest of situations. I use all the information gleaned from my investigations, especially my BBC investigation into John Schofield's death, to make these scenarios as real as possible. As we set off, with five people in the vehicle, an actor playing a fixer is driving, chatting in a foreign language. Then, without warning, we detonate a number of large barrels filled with pyrotechnics and fuel, generating a loud bang and a massive plume of smoke and flame. We also have several theatrical bullets hitting the side of the vehicle, one of which apparently strikes the driver, who is then declared dead. At this point the emphasis is on the course leader taking charge and explaining how to disembark from the vehicle. When I saw Sky News footage of journalists driving into an ambush in Ukraine, and coming under intense and direct fire, I couldn't help but think that the survival of the crew was down to the training they received, the body armour they were wearing and the good leadership shown.

***

Something has gone terribly wrong for our children. We've lost so many of them to gaming, computers, phones and social media. They no longer connect with their parents and vice versa. Too many children suffer online bullying and poor relationships that lead to self-harm, lack of self-esteem and suicide; the rise of teen suicides in Australia has been sad and alarming. Having listened to a number of parents' harrowing accounts of how they would give anything to reconnect with their children, I came up with the idea of running a Parent & Child Survival Course. After all, we have the staff, skills and equipment to deliver what I believed could be a great bonding experience. I set about pulling together a curriculum and decided to offer a course that would not only teach parents and children basic wilderness survival skills, but also include elements of our successful hostile environments training.

My first task was finding a venue and here I struck it lucky. With her husband Dan, Rachael Thornton, ace video journalist who had filmed with me on many an expedition, had a large farmstead in Richmond, at the foot of the Blue Mountains, about 65 kilometres from Sydney. When I visited them, I could not believe my luck: their property was surrounded by dense outback bush, hanging rocks and rapidly running waterways. This was exactly what I needed, and I booked it in immediately.

With a date set for the first course, which was for fathers and sons, I assembled my team. Heading up the survival skills lectures was Simon Reynolds, a fierce expeditioner and remote country wanderer. My son Tom would assist me with logistical support and a number of the dads from the Avalon community helped to keep the main HQ (Rachael and Dan's house) ticking over. Jim Palmer, a member of the ZeroRisk Intel team, played a pivotal role in securing livestock for our bush food prep demonstration.

At 12 p.m. sharp on the Friday, the first dads and kids arrived, parked and wandered over to the fire ground we'd created in front of the house. They tossed all their keys, mobile phones and computers on the table and we duly collected everything; nothing would be returned until the end of the course. I remember looking at a few long faces that day as the kids in particular realised that they were heading for a difficult few days. This first course set the pattern for all those that have followed, which have been attended by mothers and fathers, sons and daughters.

The first lecture teaches them how to build a two-person shelter out of anything they have around them. To add to the pressure, nightfall is upon them and all they have to survive on are the sleeping bags they've brought and the survival tin we've asked the parents to pack. They can bring a small tobacco-style tin containing five items, chosen from a list, which they think will help them survive; money and credit cards are not included. It's interesting to see what people bring. The parents who have researched all the items generally select the best: a small button compass, a condom for water collection, a fishing line and hooks, snares, matches, small wads of paper. We teach them to take a lighter, not matches, a number of cotton wool balls soaked in Vaseline or petroleum jelly, a flint and steel striker and a small first aid kit.

On that initial course, the dads worked feverishly to chop, snap and shave timber into small brushwood bivvies. Some got their sons involved, but others were so overwhelmed and focused that their kids were just left standing motionless, not knowing what to do. At this point, I took the dads to one side and pointed out that this was their first experience in improving communications with their kids and that they needed them to forage so they could build a shelter with a firewall in front of it. Most achieved something that would offer protection from the elements but others had to work on getting their shelters up to the standard we expected. Just as it became dark, we pulled everyone together and took them on a long walk to identify sites to place snares for rabbits and game and banks where they could fish in the fast-flowing streams. It was now time to show the dads and kids how to skin and prepare a rabbit.

What was compelling for me, as an instructor, was seeing that the dads who had been quite macho and forthright in their comments wouldn't lead from the front when it came to animal prep. In reality, most didn't possess this skill, which had somehow been lost over past generations. It was wonderful to see the sons stepping forward and taking on board all the instructions Simon was imparting. They took to the skinning and food prep and even did a first-class job of building 'dry smoker' pits to the side of their bivvies so that they could preserve the meat and protect it from animals looking for a free dinner.

As expected, all the attendees, exhausted and mentally spent, crashed in their makeshift bivvies and drifted off to sleep in the warmth of the fires burning brightly outside their shelters. The following day started with a brief inspection of their snares and fishing lines before they tended to their fires and had a strip wash in the river. As I told them, it doesn't matter where you land, you must always maintain personal hygiene as this will ensure your morale stays on track. This was something I learnt during my commando days.

Day 2 was, and still is, about picking up your survival skills. At some stage we let loose a number of live chickens, which the course members have to chase, trap and kill. They are then shown how to prepare them for cooking. Training intensifies during the day as we simulate a number of generic international travel incidents such as encountering a road traffic accident, dealing with a checkpoint and coping with aggression. This part of the training is invaluable. It really prepares them for dealing with and reacting to high-risk situations and offers the kids skills they can use later in life when they go travelling or perhaps take part in a student exchange programme.

Day 3 is the final test day. After getting up and completing the routine of checking snares and fishing hooks comes a map reading and GPS exercise. Mid-afternoon, parents and kids are briefed on the early evening task – to trek 11 kilometres on a set of given waypoints or map markers. When they arrive at the final marker, they must lie low and stay as camouflaged as possible. For the final exercise, in the dead of night, the kids assume the role of a close target recce and have to report back, to each of their parents, the exact whereabouts of the house and any observation or conversations they can hear. This information is relayed via a covert radio and discreet throat microphone.

I've been thrilled with the success of the course, which brings parents – and other relatives or guardians and so on – and children together after years spent estranged and disconnected. It's proved to be one of the most rewarding aspects of my work. Sharing experiences with your children is incredibly important. After so many years of really not being in touch, in 2018 my then 22-year-old daughter Katie and I shared the extraordinary experience of walking one of the routes that make up the famous Camino de Santiago, a network of pilgrim ways that lead to the shrine of the apostle, St James the Great, in the cathedral of Santiago de Compostela in north-west Spain. In two and a half weeks, we walked, on average, 28 kilometres a day over all kinds of terrain and in very unpredictable weather. We suffered huge blisters and dehydration and experienced highs and lows. This journey brought Katie and me back together.

EPILOGUE

AFTER MY TWO failed relationships, with Tracie and Jill, I met an Australian woman called Lisa and we had two children, Erin, born in 2007, and Tom, born in 2009. After eight years we separated. This was probably one of the lowest points of my life: suffering from a classic but awful mid-life crisis, I made some dreadful decisions and, in the end, the only thing I could do was run, hide and try to process everything that had gone on in my past.

My life has changed so much, though, since I met my partner, Kylie Palmer. She is a wonderful influence on me. She has encouraged me to slow down and take stock of my life and is also a great motivator and mentor for fitness and a healthy balanced lifestyle. We'd been together for two or three years but lived apart until 2021, when we took the plunge, sold both our properties and bought a house together by the sea. With five children between us still living at home, we've faced the usual highs and lows of a blended family and the familiar challenges of balancing home and work life. Kylie is an incredibly talented artist and designer, which led to her doing interior design work for medical and dental room fitouts. In August 2022 Kylie left her job, due to increased travel pressures and poor work/life balance and started work for me at ZeroRisk as client relationship manager. She performs this role incredibly well and has since travelled with me to Melbourne, Malaysia and Singapore to meet current and prospective clients.

As the years have passed, the risks I and my company deal with have changed. Even before the Ukraine conflict and the Covid pandemic, we started to see very different and difficult risks emerging, especially natural disasters such as floods, raging bush fires, tsunamis, earthquakes and volcanic eruptions taking their toll on the globe. Such events were considered way down the list of subjects to cover when I first sold the idea of risk assessment and management to the BBC and other media outlets.

By using every ounce of knowledge and skill gleaned from my military, BBC and ZeroRisk days, I, and my team, have helped to save countless people from the clutches of tyranny and incarceration or from severe injury and death. By imparting our experience and knowledge on a course that was initially considered unnecessary and too time consuming, and through working on the ground all over the world, we have protected everyone from members of news organisations to those working in aviation and retail and NGOs. I feel blessed to have been able to change so many people's lives for the better and to have made this dangerous world of ours a safer place.

ACKNOWLEDGEMENTS

FOR MANY YEARS this book was little more than a title, but in 2021 my fortunes changed when I met a truly inspirational and brilliant weaver of words, Emma Wilson. I owe her a huge thank you for kick-starting my writing process and sending me on my journey.

In 2022, I was fortunate to come under the expert guidance of Juliet Rogers, Managing Director of Echo Publishing. I salute her for managing me, and not getting burnt out by dealing with my rather hectic life. She deserves a medal, as does freelance editor Anna Rogers, who performed the unenviable task of whipping my story into shape. Many thanks also to the brilliant Echo team for their support.

To my truly incredible family, my mum Irene MBE and her partner Graham, my sister Angela and her husband Pete, my niece Megan, my sister-in-law Sue and her partner Dave, my nephews John and Darren, and my Uncle Pete, thank you for all your support, love and confidence in me. I'm proud and honoured to have you in my life.

To my wonderful kids, Brianna, Katie, Erin and Tom, this book is your record to share with your kids and generations to come. I hope it provides you with some insight into my decisions, many of them tough, and some inspiration and guidance, and that it prompts you to take risks and enjoy life. I haven't always been there for you all the time, but you're always in my thoughts and I adore you.

My wonderful partner Kylie has been an absolute pillar of strength and support, as I've spent endless days and nights reliving and regaling all my life stories. I love you very much and thank you for always being there for me. Thanks, too, to Kylie's kids, Koby, Jet and Clio – follow your heads and your hearts and you will have wonderful, happy lives – and to my extended family, Niki, Paul, Ellie, Soph, Kristy, Jess, Luke and Reggie, and the Hosies. I wouldn't have made it across the finish line without your endless supplies of roast dinners, laughter and banoffee pie and Ruth's homemade cakes and Colin and Kaye with their love of wine.

My formidable ZeroRisk Team have never missed a beat when stepping up to a task. The company wouldn't be what it is without you. I'd therefore like to thank all those, past and present, who have helped me to achieve this success: Lisa Birch, Andy Bolt, Rachael Branch, Matt Cardinaels, the late Matt Carr, Charles Carter, Jon Cherney, Chris Clarke, Sue Clarke, Francis Cox, Kabir Dhanji, Scott Dullard, Jas Ellery, Ray Floro, Gordy, Tom Hanley, Tim Hayes, Brendon Hempel, Will Hosie, Richard James, Paul Jones, Jude Kendal, Owen Lawrence, Remy Lowe, Grant McKay, Phil Milligan, Naz, Jade Nolan, Jason Owen, Jim Palmer, Ajit Patel, Richard Patton, John Pickering, Gary Preston, Chris Pritchard, Simon Reynolds, Jamie Ross, Tom Riches, Jeremy Rowsell, Kirsty Rushmore, Liam Ryan, Rob Simpson, Tom Sullivan (Sully), Greg and Charlene Symmonds, Paul Warrington, Emma Wilson, Greg Waters, Bec Wilken, Sam Young, Andy Young, Ting Zhang and too many more to mention.

For the past 20 years I've frequently been embedded with Agence

France-Presse (AFP) Asia and have had the pleasure of working with some extremely brave and talented local journalists. I've always had complete support from the AFP senior management team of Phil Chetwynd, Emmanuel Duparcq, Giles Hewitt, Peter Cunliffe Jones, Marc Lavine, Pedro Ugarte and Eric Wishart, and they have always listened to and acted upon my safety advice.

To the Kmart/Target Senior Management team, past and present, Tracie Walker, Guy Russo, Ian Bailey, Arjun Puri, Asker Lauberg, Deb, Dipti and Ruby, thank you for trusting in our continued support following the 2016 Holy Artisan Attack and recent Covid crisis. As with all our other Australian retail clients, Mike Schneider (Bunnings), Adrian Barratt (Just Group), Sheila Oenning and Suzie Learmonth (Workwear Group), and Cameron Newell, Andy Cooper and Sean Higgins (Coles), it's been an honour to serve, protect and be with you as your company travels the globe.

Huge thanks to David Anderson and Chris Oliver Taylor (ABC), for believing in me when I stepped foot on Australian soil in 2003, offering me the chance to use my skills and supporting me over many years. To ABC's Steve Murray and Manda Hatter, it has been an honour and a privilege to have worked with you on many crazy and often hazardous TV, film and studio projects.

I salute each and every one of my former BBC colleagues, in particular Mike Reason and Peter Hunter (who gave me a huge career break), Jenny Baxter, the late Eric Bowman, Jeremy Bowen, Ben Brown, Nick Bryant, the late Chris Cramer, Paul Danahar, George Eykyn, Peter Greste, Issam Ikirmawi, Colin Jones, Sarah Ward Lilley, Clive Myrie, Richard Sambrook, Dee Simpson, John Simpson, Vin Ray, Fran Unsworth, Adrian Van Klaveren and Morwen Williams.

They say that the company you keep can make you as a person, and I couldn't have wished for a more loyal, trusting and influential bunch of guys and girls than those I worked alongside during my time in the Royal Naval Medical Branch, Royal Marines M&AW Cadre and 42 Commando. Per Mare Per Terram – until the final RV.